Cha... ...s
in Primary Education

Also available from Bloomsbury

Developing Teacher Expertise, edited by Margaret Sangster
Early Numeracy, Margaret Sangster and Rona Catterall
Readings for Reflective Teaching in Schools, edited by Andrew Pollard
Reflective Teaching in Schools, Andrew Pollard
Readings for Reflective Teaching in Early Education, edited by Jennifer Colwell and Andrew Pollard
Reflective Teaching in Early Education, Jennifer Colwell

Challenging Perceptions in Primary Education

Exploring Issues in Practice

Edited by
Margaret Sangster

Bloomsbury Academic
An imprint of Bloomsbury Publishing Plc

BLOOMSBURY
LONDON • NEW DELHI • NEW YORK • SYDNEY

Bloomsbury Academic
An imprint of Bloomsbury Publishing Plc

50 Bedford Square	1385 Broadway
London	New York
WC1B 3DP	NY 10018
UK	USA

www.bloomsbury.com

BLOOMSBURY and the Diana logo are trademarks of Bloomsbury Publishing Plc

First published 2015

British Library Cataloguing-in-Publication Data
A catalogue record for this book is available from the British Library.

ISBN: HB: 978-1-4725-7838-9
     PB: 978-1-4725-7837-2
  ePDF: 978-1-4725-7840-2
  ePub: 978-1-4725-7839-6

Library of Congress Cataloging-in-Publication Data
[INSERT HERE]

Typeset by Deanta Global Publishing Services, Chennai, India
Printed and bound in India

Contents

Contents **vii**

List of contributors

Rebecca Austin is Senior Lecturer at Canterbury Christ Church University, UK, where she leads the Primary English Team. She worked in primary schools in Kent before becoming a lecturer in Primary English promoting children's literature as central to children's development as readers, writers and talkers. Her research interests include learning outside the classroom and the use of popular culture in schools. She is currently studying and researching the role of the media in adolescents' identity formation.

Jonathan Barnes is Senior Lecturer at Canterbury Christ Church University, UK, and has 30 years of classroom experience, and a love of the arts which power his commitment to cross-curricular approaches. As a head he devised a curriculum based on the school locality. He now researches links between cross-curricular/creative approaches and well-being. He is the author of *Cross-Curricular Learning 3-14* (2011) and teaches about exploring and creating environments as well as music in education. His recent research interests include linking involvement in the arts with the well-being of children.

Karl Bentley is Senior Lecturer in Computing and Education and Academic Studies at Canterbury Christ Church University, UK, as well as link tutoring students in school. He was a school-based ICT Advanced Skills Teacher before entering higher education. His main interests are the implementation of the new Computing Curriculum and the use of interactive technologies to deliver university course content.

Graham Birrell is Senior Lecturer in the Department for Postgraduate Initial Teacher Education at Canterbury Christ Church University, UK. He is responsible for Primary History in the Faculty of Education and has a particular interest in education policy. Before entering higher education he taught in several primary schools across Kent. He is currently very interested in the role of social media, particularly blogging, in education.

Andy Bloor is Senior Lecturer and primary lead in Special Educational Needs at Canterbury Christ Church University, UK. He has worked almost two decades in the field of education, much of it working closely with children with special educational needs, specifically those with social, emotional and behavioural difficulties. He is currently a reviewer on the journals *Emotional and Behavioural Difficulties* and *ADHD in Practice*. He is also the Education Officer on the National Executive for the Social, Emotional and Behavioural Difficulties Association.

Anthony Clarke is Senior Lecturer teaching Professional Studies and Primary Languages at Canterbury Christ Church University, UK, and manages several exchange programmes with universities across Europe. He has been both a deputy head and a head teacher of primary schools in Kent and has a particular interest in international education systems and developing students' language and cultural awareness. He works closely with local schools as a link tutor and provides support for the development of primary languages.

Peter Dorman was Principal Lecturer at Canterbury Christ Church University, UK, and has had a long and varied career in primary education. He has worked in schools, for local education authorities and more lately as a university lecturer. He taught ICT and Professional Studies but was also involved in the Cross-curricular module. His interests include the effective use of ICT with pupils with Additional Educational Needs, learning in global contexts and the professional development of Newly Qualified Teachers.

Aidan Gillespie is Senior Lecturer in Primary Education at Canterbury Christ Church University, UK, and the subject lead for Primary Religious Education. He is currently researching how teachers both understand and express their spirituality across a variety of primary education settings. His interests include inter-faith dialogue and how Religious Education assists students in challenging educational and cultural assumptions.

Michael Green was Programme Director for the BA in Primary Education at Canterbury Christ Church University, UK, and leads the undergraduate work on learning outside the classroom. His interests include children's use of technology and the opportunities and barriers for children to learn outside the classroom. Prior to joining Initial Teacher Education he was an assistant head teacher in a large primary school in Medway. He now works in Partnership at Greenwich University.

Peter Gregory is Senior Lecturer at Canterbury Christ Church University, UK, and has taught across all phases and sectors of education in London and the South East. He was originally trained in ceramics before teaching in a number of schools and other settings. He held several school leadership and local authority advisory roles before teaching on a range of initial teacher education programmes in London and Kent. He is currently both Vice President of the National Society of Education in Art and Design and a European Representative on the World Council of the International Society for Education Through Art.

Sue Hammond is Senior Lecturer at Canterbury Christ Church University, UK, and has spent more than 20 years teaching in primary schools across the Foundation Stage, Key Stage 1 and 2. She cares passionately about young children's learning and opportunities and leads specialist Early Years courses for student teachers. She has led trips to India for students and newly qualified teachers. She has also worked with primary education tutors in Malaysia. She has spoken at international conferences and is currently researching children's early social development and learner identity.

Mark Hardman is Senior Lecturer at Canterbury Christ Church University, UK, focusing on science education. He also runs teacher education and science outreach programmes from Imperial College London, UK, and is tutor on the Teach First programme at Canterbury Christ Church University, UK. He is a specialist in physics education and his research interest is focused on complexity theory within education.

Claire Hewlett is Senior Lecturer at Canterbury Christ Church University, UK, focusing on primary art, science, cross curricular approaches and professional studies. She previously taught in primary schools. She is particularly interested in how Art can be used to support learning across all areas of the curriculum, particularly how Art can be used as a vehicle for children to express their wider learning and understanding. She believes in taking an active learning approach to teaching.

Gill Hope is Senior Lecturer in Design and Technology Education at Canterbury Christ Church University, UK. She has written research articles and journal articles as well as authored three books on the subject, including *Thinking and Learning through Drawing* (2008). She has worked with primary education tutors in Malaysia and in 2013 she was a member of the consultation group for the new 2014 National Curriculum for Design and Technology.

Kristy Howells is Senior Lecturer at Canterbury Christ Church University, UK, focusing on primary physical education and professional studies, as well as link tutoring students in school nationally and internationally. She currently leads an innovative part-time primary education programme specializing in the 7 to 11 age range and lectures on Physical Education and Sports Sciences degrees. Her particular area of research expertise is physical activity.

Chloe Lever is a third-year student studying BA (Hons) in Primary Education at Canterbury Christ Church University, UK, specializing in Diversity and Participation. Through volunteering in different schools, Chloe has used her passion for dance to encourage creativity in young learners. As part of her professional development, Chloe spent one month teaching in a rural government school in Machakos, Kenya.

Tony Mahon is Senior Lecturer at Canterbury Christ Church University, UK, focusing on primary English, English as an Additional Language and education and academic studies. He also has responsibility for organizing international placements for student teachers. He has worked as a teacher and teacher educator in England, Egypt, Saudi Arabia, Philippines, Japan and Hong Kong and is currently a consultant for World Bank Projects in Palestine. Academic interests include the pedagogy of English as an Additional Language, multicultural education and international development education.

Claire March is Senior Lecturer at Canterbury Christ Church University, UK, focusing on primary art and design, science and professional studies to students across a range of pathways and programmes. She also has a role as a partnership development leader which enables her to work closely in partnership with a range of schools. She has worked as a primary teacher for a number of years leading subject development within school and beyond. Her research interests are linked to art and design and the role technology can play within this area.

Jill Matthews was Senior Lecturer at Canterbury Christ Church University, UK. She has both secondary and primary teaching experience and, within the primary sector she has held subject responsibility posts for science, mathematics, literacy and primary languages. Moving in to higher education, she taught science and mathematics as well as being a member of the undergraduate management team. Her interests include the role language plays in developing children's mathematical understanding and creating an inclusive learning environment.

Jason Mellor is Senior Lecturer in Primary Education at Canterbury Christ Church University, UK, teaching English and professional studies to students across a range of pathways and programmes. He has over 20 years of experience within primary education and has been both a leading teacher in partnership with the local authority and a deputy head teacher. He also supports the development of in-school mentoring for student teachers. His research interests include assessment for learning, analysis of education policy and the role of faith and religion within education.

Coral Newton is a third-year student studying BA (Hons) in Primary Education at Canterbury Christ Church University, UK, specializing in Advanced Early Years. Prior to her training she completed a CACHE Diploma in Child Care and Education and spent three years as a teaching assistant in both key stages. As part of her alternative placement, Coral spent one month teaching in a rural government school in Machakos, Kenya.

John-Paul Riordan is Senior Lecturer in Primary Education at Canterbury Christ Church University, UK, and teaches secondary science part-time in a school for children who have learning difficulties. He has been a teacher for 15 years. His research interests include instructional strategy, conceptual change in science and religious education and inclusion.

Margaret Sangster was Principal Lecturer in Primary Mathematics and Professional Studies at Canterbury Christ Church University, UK, as well as a link tutor with schools. She has worked in a number of primary and middle schools as an advisory teacher for mathematics before entering higher education where she held several management posts. She has visited Malaysia several times to work with primary education tutors. Her particular interests are children learning mathematics, teachers' and students' classroom practice and how to encourage children's independent learning.

Victoria Schulze is Senior Lecturer at Canterbury Christ Church University, UK, where she focuses on primary languages and professional studies. As Primary Language team lead, she also manages undergraduate and postgraduate provision. She is also involved in an extensive exchange scheme of teacher trainees across several European countries and other EU projects, link tutoring students in schools here and in Germany. She has taught across the 5 to 11 age-range in a number of primary schools before entering higher education. Her particular interests are pupil motivation and integrating languages into the wider curriculum.

Stephen Scoffham is Principal Lecturer at Canterbury Christ Church University, UK, and an advisor/consultant for school atlases and the author of many primary school geography texts. His interests include creativity, sustainability, environmental education and global perspectives. He is currently director of Canterbury Christ Church University's *Futures Initiative*, which aims to develop sustainability perspectives in all areas of academic life. He is also honorary publications officer for the Geographical Association and a trustee of a local development education centre (WEDG).

Paula Stone is Senior Lecturer at Canterbury Christ Church University, UK, and teaches Primary Mathematics education at both undergraduate and postgraduate levels with particular responsibility for the Mathematics Research Module. She is an associate of the NCETM and contributes regularly to publications including writing for Primary Magazine. The research focus for her PhD is 'How can we sustain the academic in Initial Teacher Education'.

Caroline Tancock is Senior Lecturer at Canterbury Christ Church University, UK, and member of the BA (Hons) in Primary Education management team. She teaches many modules on the undergraduate programme including English and Professional Studies and on the full-time PGCE English course. Her current research interests include cultural influences upon reading experiences and attitudes.

Karen Vincent is Programme Director for the Primary Education Progression Route at Canterbury Christ Church University, UK, and teaches across many of the programmes, both undergraduate and postgraduate, specializing in Early Years education. She also teaches Professional Studies and link tutors students on their school placements. Before moving into higher education she worked as a teacher for many years across all age phases. Her research interests include young children's perceptions of learning, the transition between Reception and Year 1 (4–6-year-olds) as well as self-study of pedagogies in teacher education.

Rosemary Walters is Senior Lecturer at Canterbury Christ Church University, UK. She has a background in teaching Religious Education and History and has been a Local Authority Religious Education Support Teacher and a Cathedral Schools Officer before working with primary initial teacher education students focusing on these two subject areas. She has a special interest in the role of spiritual development and the concept of transformative education.

Terry Whyte is Senior Lecturer at Canterbury Christ Church University, UK, focusing on primary geography, global studies and professional studies as well as link tutoring students in school. He chairs one of the regional partnership groups who meet to discuss students' school experiences. He has worked in a number of primary schools before entering higher education. His interests are students understanding and awareness of their environment, their world around them and developing children's geographical skills.

Viv Wilson is Principal Lecturer at Canterbury Christ Church University, UK, focusing on research methods and professional studies. She has worked in primary and secondary schools before entering higher education as a lecturer in educational drama. She has considerable experience of working in international teacher training settings. Her current interests include mentoring, students' professional learning in schools, and supporting teachers as school-based researchers.

Vanessa Young is Principal Lecturer at Canterbury Christ Church University, UK, focusing on primary music and professional studies and was programme director of a highly thought of 7–14 teacher training programme for 10 years. She has a particular interest in the curriculum and the aims of education. She has worked in a number of primary schools and also has extensive experience in staff development both in a local authority and in higher education. Her writing and research focuses on aspects of teacher development.

Preface

Have you ever thought about why you make the decisions you do make as a teacher? What influences your teaching style? You will have adopted methods received in your training and used ideas you have discussed and read. You only have to observe other people teach to realize that there are many different styles of teaching. Maybe there are elements in your teaching of how you were taught yourself. Maybe you have styled your teaching on people you have worked with. This book sets out to inform and also to engage you in reflecting on your own practice, even challenging it.

The chapters in this book, a follow on from *Developing Teacher Expertise: Exploring Key Issues in Primary Practice*, continue to ask questions about teaching primary school children. The book is divided into five parts; Creating a good learning environment, Developing an effective curriculum, Using imagery in teaching, Learning from education in other countries, and Exploring wider perspectives on education.

The contributors are all linked to Canterbury Christ Church University which is an institution deeply engaged in teacher education, through training students, working with schools, colleges and early years establishments, researching many aspects of education, and promoting primary education not only in the region but also in other countries. The short, focused articles would be ideal as pre-reading as well as follow-up reading to seminars, tutorials and group discussions. The articles are designed to challenge your thinking, the intention being to promote reflection and debate.

Canterbury Christ Church University is keen that all teachers seek to become reflective and reflexive practitioners. The ideas presented here may or may not have been in the compass of your experience but by turning a mirror on your own teaching in the light of what you have read, it is hoped that you will be better informed about your own decision-making, explore your own actions and consequently become a more effective teacher.

Introduction

Everyone has experienced education and therefore everyone will have an opinion on education. This opinion will be based on what worked and did not work for them, or what they did not experience but perceive as better. These opinions are formed early on in life and quite often are very secure; one might even use the word 'entrenched'; long-held views often emerge during discussions between students and between teachers. It is understandable that people draw upon their personal experience of education but effective education is bigger than a single person's experience. A significant aspect of teacher education courses is to offer different experiences and the views of others so that the learner can reflect on the purposes of and the methods used in education. This is done through placement experience, discussion of theory and research, further study, reading and talking to peers and colleagues. It cannot be underestimated how important reflection on one's own actions is when developing professional skills and understanding.

As a result of the way opinions are formed, have you sensed that there is an unspoken assumption that the education of the past is appropriate for the children of the present? Is this appropriate? There exists the present age in which we live as adults and children live in that age too but they will also live in a future age as adults. A 5-year-old will begin his or her adult life in 13 years' time. What will the world be like then and what will be different? Many things will be the same and many will be different. We only have to look at the technology revolution in the past 10 years to realize how much things can change. How do we prepare children for this future adult world, while at the same time meet the needs of their current children's world? How do we ensure that their educational experience is a captivating learning experience in a distracting world – an experience which will, if successful, motivate them to continue to learn for the rest of their life? Successful people are adaptive, prepared to take the initiative, think for themselves and make informed decisions. Would we not wish this for all of the children we educate? And should not these be the expectations for young children as well as teenagers?

There is a sense that all that is required of primary schools is that children leave being able to read, write and do arithmetic. True, these should be the main goals but education is so much more. Should they not be acceptable members of society, be able to work together, know where and how to find out information and consider its worth, solve problems, be informed, be tolerant of others, be fit and interested in participating in many activities? In a partnership between parents, school and the child much of this can be achieved as long as those involved are in agreement about these aims.

The current zeitgeist suggests that learning is a discipline which can be crafted by the teacher and therefore teaching is a craft-based activity and as such children can be trained like apprentices. There are elements of schooling which fit with a training mode such as good behaviour patterns, learning certain core pieces of knowledge and key skills. But there, I suggest, the parallel ends. Good schools seek to develop all their individuals to reason, to cope with a wide range of life experiences, to be successful in a variety of subjects and to make unique contributions to their own education. The ultimate desire for success must come from within the child if it is to be sustained through life.

Consider the educational setting: school authority does not extend outside the walls of the school; within school, thankfully, there are few stringent punishments; education is a partnership with parents who may not share the same values; there are no volunteers, all must participate; no one can be thrown out of the system; all are expected to be successful. Viewed in this way, teaching and learning become a challenge, both for the teacher and for the child. This is where the strength of the teacher enters the mix. Beyond policy, syllabii and rules each teacher is unique; unique in their interpretation of education, unique in their procedural choices and unique in their relationships with the children in their class. The teacher offers a subtle mix of knowledge, skills and perception about children. He or she has the strength of craft which underpins the function of teaching but the choice of how and when to introduce, expand, respond, challenge, even the ability to keep quiet and listen; recognizing when it is appropriate to work as a whole class and when to tailor the work to groups or work with individuals. Teaching is a nurturing job, encouraging children's minds and personalities to grow and function in a complex society. One could argue that it is imperative that teachers remain informed and willing to evolve their practice in this ever-changing world in which we and the adults of the future live.

The chapters in the five sections in this book cover several aspects of primary education. All of them suggest that teachers have choices. What will your choices be?

Creating a good learning environment

Jonathan Barnes provides an excellent introduction to this section by examining 12 principles across five environmental headings which he feels should be present in the primary classroom. He refers to the physical values, social, emotional and cultural environments and explores how they can be promoted in the classroom. This theme continues with a consideration of the school ethos when Rosemary Walters discusses the idea of 'Schools with Souls'. Her view is that deep learning and a comprehensive education will occur when spiritual, moral, social and cultural issues are addressed. A moral issue can arise, as Andy Bloor points out when he unpicks the relationship between the specialist special needs teacher and the classroom teacher. How can both the roles be utilized to the advantage of the child?

In England there is lively debate about the balance of play and formal learning provided in classes for 5-year-olds. At the heart of this debate are the following questions: 'How do children learn'? and 'What learning can take place when children play'? Karen Vincent offers a strong case for the inclusion of play in the curriculum in the early years. This attunes with Gill Hope's chapter on practical work. Again, we see a difficult balance between the time-consuming practical activities and the more formal didactic approach. She uses the subject of design and technology to illustrate the possible learning which can occur when children engage in practical activities.

There is little dispute about the benefits of school visits. Michael Green takes us outside the classroom, not to consider the value of school visits to children but to the teacher. Based on reports that visits are time-consuming and risky, his hope is that teachers will see the benefit to their own professional development.

Back in the classroom, the next two chapters in this section take an enlightened view of classroom behaviour. Mark Hardman turns the focus on the 'messiness' and 'complexity' of learning and the challenge of matching this to a linear curriculum, while John-Paul Riordan asks us if teachers practise the art of deception. Finally, and linked to many of the points made by Mark, Margaret Sangster has another look at assessment claims. To what extent does assessment 'ensure' that children are learning? She asks if this is not too big a claim on the role of assessment.

Developing an effective curriculum

When you begin to lose something you value, you begin to quantify its contribution. This is a theme throughout this section. As the 'squeeze' on the curriculum in England narrows it towards an emphasis on the core subjects of English (first language teaching), mathematics and science, the evidence is building about the contribution of other subjects to children's learning. Many of these chapters point out the value of qualities more difficult to assess, qualities which 'almost silently' underpin us as functional, educated human beings.

Jonathan Barnes returns to the theme of social and emotional development but this time in the context of the arts. He draws upon evidence from government reports, research and prominent theorists to make a case for the arts to remain in the curriculum as they promote well-being alongside many skills. He supports theory and research with four revealing case studies. This makes for a very persuasive case for retaining art in the curriculum.

Geography, another subject which could be marginalized, also has much to offer children according to Terry Whyte. He points out how much geography is integrated into our everyday lives and how much the poorer we would be without it. We would also be worse off if we abolished break times and Kristy Howells argues that break times make a significant contribution to children's education. Not only does this time contribute to children's physical health but also gives opportunities for social development. She also examines evidence of exactly how much physical activity boys and girls undertake during break times. With growing concerns about obesity in the western world, she shows that we would do well to value the contribution of break times.

Back in the classroom Jill Matthews has mathematics under the microscope but not in the usual way. She asks us to consider the importance of language in developing mathematical understanding. Mathematics is an invented language and as such should it not be treated with more oral discussion and more social activity? Contexts, images, connections to real life have a contribution to make to children's understanding of mathematics. This idea is picked up later by Victoria Schulz in her chapter on the need to immerse children in second language learning. She argues for an integrated approach to language learning as opposed to discrete lessons. She sees effective teaching of language as 'frequent, rich, holistic, real life and sensory'.

Finally, Stephen Scoffham moves us to a bigger issue – that of climate change and global warming. Should primary children be taught about these things? Children will inherit the future world so one could argue that yes, they have a right to know and Stephen argues that it is better to address this subject in school and allay fears than for children to piece together fragments of media sensationalism.

Using imagery in teaching

Throughout the world the classroom environment varies. This is partly due to the economics of education and partly to do with the prevailing philosophies. In England the primary classroom is usually full of visual imagery and recently this has been added to by the access to the WorldWide Web. Projectors throw multitudes of images up on to the screen to support and inform lessons; children themselves have unprecedented access to the internet both at home and school. This has to have an impact on teaching and children's learning. Have we, as yet, realized the impact? The chapters in this section open the door on some of the emerging issues.

The first chapter by Karl Bentley forms a revealing introduction to this section with a serious consideration of the biological science behind the effect of images, their retention and their role in learning. Peter Gregory urges us to teach children to look more closely at their world – something which could easily be lost in the snowstorm of whirling images presented to children today. He asks to what extent children's visual literacy is developed.

Taking time to explore is another recurring theme, which reappears in Claire Hewlett and Claire March's chapter on the use of electronic programs for art. Are they a shortcut to drawing and painting or have they more to offer? Claire and Claire bring out the tensions between traditional approaches to art in school and the possibilities now on offer as a result of the technological revolution reaching the classroom.

Aidan Gillespie picks up the theme of visual literacy again but this time in the context of religious education. How can images support children's understanding of religion and an understanding of their own cultural context? To quote Aidan, this technology 'leads us into some challenging waters but also well-springs of opportunity and potential'.

Learning from education in other countries

Chloe Lever and Coral Newton open their chapter with these lines drawn from Emert (2008), 'We are all part of an ever-changing, developing global community and perhaps, as educators, we should prepare children for the future and teach them to be productive members of society by understanding and respecting differences from a global perspective'. I could not say it better; it offers a rationale for reflecting on the international experiences of both students and tutors working in other countries. Sue Hammond and Anthony Clarke begin to unwrap aspects of educational visits abroad followed by some serious questions from Tony Mahon about why we are there at all. The two undergraduates, Chloe and Coral explain what they learnt from a short-term teaching experience in Kenya before Caroline Tancock whisks us away to India. In this chapter, she examines the development of primary education in India, using it to underpin her argument about transferability. Finally, Viv Wilson challenges us again to consider what we, as teachers, really learn from such educational visits.

Exploring wider perspectives on education

Within this section the chapters cover a wide range of topics but common to all of them is the thought provoking questions they raise about our attitude to education. Some deep-seated beliefs are challenged here but ultimately you, as teachers, develop your own beliefs which in turn inform your practice. Here are some chapters which will hopefully get you thinking about fundamental issues.

The first two chapters are a counter-argument to the idea that good teaching can be accomplished without reference to either research or theory. Vanessa Young gives good reasons for developing practice within a theoretical context and Paula Stone argues for the use of research to inform practice. This could be the research of others or your own research. She offers a model of classroom research which benefits the teacher and can be purposeful and accomplished within the restrains of a busy teacher's schedule. Both writers are seeking a profession where teachers are reflective and reflexive.

Rebecca Austin and Graham Birrell are interested in the influence of political decisions on education and in this chapter discuss how teachers respond to this situation without promoting the ideologies and views associated with political parties. In many countries education cannot be divorced from government influence. Is it safe for teachers to take a critical stance on political policy? Linked to this, Jill Matthews questions whether party political influence is helping or hampering English education and whether we might do better to follow the example of other countries' more neutral systems.

Who do we learn from? Peter Dorman provides an interesting chapter on the differences between a role model and a mentor. This leads us to consider where we get our inspiration from, how we develop our beliefs and how we choose to act in the classroom. There is plenty of food for reflection here. Rebecca Austin returns with a chapter questioning why teachers are often reluctant to take risks in their practice. What are the perceived and actual restraints and, importantly, what effect is this having on children growing up in a 'protected' environment?

The chapters in this book are wide ranging and each is meant to be used as a starting point for discussion. It is hoped that they will enable readers to reflect on and enhance their own professional practice.

Part I
Creating a Good Learning Environment

A successful learning environment is one in which all children in a class can progress in their learning. There are many ways to set up a classroom environment that is stimulating for children. The social, emotional and physical welfare of children as well as their academic abilities have to be considered for children to feel secure and motivated. Part 1 asks some key questions about how you run your classroom.

Can individual teachers build a successful learning environment for children?

Jonathan Barnes

1

We respond to settings in highly personal ways. Each of us, even identical twins sharing the same physical, social and emotional surroundings, according to Pinker occupies 'a unique environment' (Pinker 2003). How then can an individual teacher create in their classroom an environment that is likely to promote learning for all children?

Factors well beyond school affect the moods, attitudes, aptitudes and readiness to learn that we bring to the classroom. It is unlikely that any environment will engage everyone, but there are principles that if applied in classrooms make it more likely that children will be motivated, involved and supported in their learning journey. These principles fall under five environmental headings; the values environment; the physical environment; the social environment; the emotional environment and the cultural environment.

Can you give an example of each from your own practice?

The environments mentioned above overlap and are interdependent. Teachers are involved in constructing and controlling each of them – usually without thinking about it. It is important that teachers should carefully consider the environments they preside over, what they want them to be like and how they can promote learning for all. Let us consider each in detail.

In the **values environment** a value is a fundamental belief that acts as a spur to action (Booth and Ainscow 2011). Each of us arrives at any setting with a distinct set of values that influence our decisions, large or small. For children, actions as insignificant as picking up a pencil or as important as entering the learning journey, is a result of their emergent values and those of the people around them. Teachers may find their values conflict with those of their pupils, but as highly influential adults they can establish a shared system of values that significantly impact on the children's self-image, relationships and attitudes to learning. They can help create a setting where the chances of each child having an affirmative experience are significantly higher than them having a negative one. Negotiation is the key to ensuring those values are jointly owned.

Has there been a time when your values were at variance with those of a pupil? How did you resolve the situation?

Principle 1: Negotiate and express shared class values in simple language. As a teacher, you might write up to five shared values that will apply across all situations and are constantly referred to in the classroom. They should be discussed at length, be open to revision, repeated at least daily and also shared with parents. Use inclusive language and avoid negatives; for example, we care for each other, we listen to each other, we follow instructions first time, we are fair. The relevant value(s) should be named and acknowledged when any curricular, pedagogical, relational and organizational decisions are made.

Principle 2: Ensure that values are ever-present and that children and adults in the room refer to them frequently.

In considering the **physical environment**, our surroundings and objects within them influence our mood, even our perceptions. From a neurological perspective, Damasio claims that, 'few objects in the world are emotionally neutral,' (2003: 56), suggesting that the furniture, decoration, equipment, even the view from a classroom window can have a unique and highly personal impact on our thinking. When objects mean something subtly different to each person, then particular artefacts, constructional or decorative details, the trees in the playground or the spiders under the windowsill can become rich sources of engagement. If Damasio's claim is true, then an impromptu field trip to the playground wild area might have transformative potential for a child.

How do suggestions regarding the emotional power of inanimate objects influence thinking about our classrooms?

Each object is capable of generating connections. Therefore, the more displays and exhibitions enhance classroom walls and spaces, the more children work outside, the more interesting objects are brought into the class, the greater the chances of engagement. Diverse, multi-faceted experiences that speak to all the senses, making connections across the whole brain, are seen by neuroscientists as the fundamental prerequisites of school learning (Goswami and Bryant 2007).

Principle 3: Mount and change classroom displays and exhibitions frequently.

Principle 4: Arrange for frequent experiences with objects to generate physical connections with subjects across the curriculum.

Principle 5: Use the view, playground, corridors and school building as a learning resource.

In considering the **social environment** we need to accept that we are social learners. The ancients, Plato, Socrates and Aristotle knew the power of social learning; Vygotsky (1978) reaffirmed this through psychology. Today neuroscience adds its voice to the evidence for learning through relationships (Goswami and Bryant 2007). The knowledge that most of us learn most effectively with and through others, should profoundly impact upon classroom organization. In primary schools, it is common to see tables arranged in groups. This practice is increasingly challenged as pressures mount to meet subject knowledge targets rather than goals linked to deeper understanding.

How are the tables arranged in your classroom? Why have you chosen this formation?

There is no right way to arrange the desks and chairs in a classroom – it depends upon the kind of learning required. Flexibility is the key. Teachers should be relaxed about rearranging the furniture: a circle of chairs for music, groups for geography, history and science analysis and observation, perhaps rows for art and design technology, around the perimeter of the room for computing or in pairs for creative speaking, listening and writing.

Principle 6: Be flexible about classroom furniture; move it a lot.

The social world of the school starts at the school gates. The greeting parents/carers get as they enter school premises, a teacher's friendly comments on new shoes, lost teeth or birthday parties as children enter the room, significantly contribute to the secure atmosphere argued to be conducive to thinking and acting creatively (Halpin 2003: 110–11). Care, kindness, fairness, gratitude, honesty or other positive behaviour may illustrate the core values of the class. As a teacher displays and draws attention to examples of such behaviour, they build a social environment that is affirmative, sensitive and safe for all. Within a predictable positive social community, even children with complex barriers to learning make significant progress (Barnes 2014).

Principle 7: Relate social expectations to the core values of the class.

Principle 8: Consistently identify and praise examples of good social behaviour.

The **emotional environment** overlaps with the social. Personal emotions direct behaviour, control learning, define relationships and profoundly influence health and well-being (Immordino-Yang and Damasio 2007). Unfortunately the arts, which identify, exercise and develop emotions like empathy and sensitivity, are often marginalized in systems that overemphasize simple knowledge acquisition. MacGilchrist (2010), from a neuroscientific perspective, suggests that individual well-being relies upon a balance between the 'right brain' activities, that connect individuals emotionally to self, others, things and places, and the 'left brain' approaches that are more dispassionate, logical, structural and mechanical.

What balance do you think you achieve in your curriculum?

Principle 9: Aim at a broad and balanced curriculum that moves towards equal value for all curriculum subjects.

Principle 10: Allow opportunities for both emotional and mechanical or dispassionate responses.

When we are happy we learn better. Neuroscientists (Damasio 2003; Immordino-Yang and Faeth 2010) claim that positive emotions provide optimal conditions for learning. Positivity also appears to broaden and build our ability to make relationships, think creatively, integrate past experience with the present and extend our physical and mental abilities (Fredrickson 2009). Both motivation and disaffection have emotional starting points; therefore, if we want to promote learning we need to work towards an emotional environment of security, trust, curiosity, enthusiasm and engagement.

Principle 11: Foster positive emotional connection as a prerequisite for learning.

How might you improve the emotional environment of your classroom?

Each child belongs to many cultures. 'The shared values and patterns of behaviour that characterize different social groups and communities' (National Advisory Committee on Creative and Cultural Education (1999: 47)) probably develop to provide the security of belonging. If teachers want their children to identify with the culture of the classroom, the environment should relate to the other cultures that children belong to: family, faith or friendship group, social class or ethnic background. Relationship to other less well-defined cultures – 'high culture', 'British culture', 'intellectual culture' – may be profitably established through gentle exposure, visits and visitors, but generally after a child's 'home' culture has been recognized and honoured.

Every class develops its own culture. By establishing shared values, a supportive social and emotional climate and a commonly appreciated space, a teacher would already have started establishing a distinctive and positive culture. Cultures are also affected by attitudes and choices. A classroom environment that encourages questioning, exploration, debating and supported risk-taking will, according to the constructivists, build a culture conducive to intellectual growth and achievement (see Bruner 1961; Freire 1984; Dewey 1997). The chances of any child in such a class feeling a failure should be low.

What cultural aspects do you value and promote in your classroom?

Connections are central to deep, transferable learning. I have argued elsewhere (Barnes 2015) that it is easier to help a child participate in a wider culture when they are linked socially, philosophically, morally, or through arts, sports and language to the world beyond the classroom. Engagement with the wider world may involve confronting complex and difficult issues bigger than the curriculum itself – environment, faith, community, sustainability, peace, social justice – Alexander (2010) and others (Freire 1984; Kohlberg 1988) maintain that the rewards are great. When physical, social, emotional and cultural environments align within a strong moral purpose, learning is not just effective; it has a meaning, a direction and a goal.

Principle 12: Make and sustain multiple links with representatives of the local community and to local and national institutions to develop the sense of belonging to an affirmative and inclusive culture.

References and further reading

Alexander, R. (2010), *Children, Their World, Their Education*. Cambridge: Cambridge University Press.

Barnes, J. (2014), 'Drama to promote well-being with 6 and 7 years olds with communication difficulties: The Speech Bubbles Project', *Perspectives in Public Health*, 134, (2), 103–9.

—(2015), *Cross-Curricular Learning 3–14*. London: Sage.

Berkowitz, M. and Oser, F. (eds) (1985), *Moral Education: Theory and Application*. Hillsdale, NJ: Erlbaum.

Booth, T. and Ainscow, M. (2011), *The Index for Inclusion*. Bristol: Centre for Studies in Inclusive Education.

Bruner, J. (1961), 'The act of discovery', *Harvard Educational Review*, 31, (1), 21–32.

Damasio, A. (2003), *Looking for Spinoza: Joy Sorrow and the Feeling Brain*. New York: Harcourt.

Dewey, J. (1997), *How We Think*. New York: Dover Publications.

Fredrickson, B. (2009), *Positivity*. New York: Crown.

Freire, P. (1984), *Pedagogy of the Oppressed*. New York: Continuum.

Goswami, U. and Bryant, P. (2007), *Children's Cognitive Development and Learning* (Primary Review Survey, 2/A). Cambridge: University of Cambridge Faculty of Education.

Halpin, D. (2003), *Hope and Education: The Role of the Utopian Imagination*. London: Routledge-Falmer.

Immordino-Yang, M. and Faeth, M. (2010), in D. Sousa, D. Ansari and J. Christodoulou (eds), *Mind, Brain, & Education: Neuroscience Implications for the Classroom*, Chapter 4. Bloomington, IL: Solution Tree Press, 69–84.

Kohlberg, L. (1988), 'The just community approach to moral education in theory and practice', *Journal of Moral Education*, 17, (3), 195–208.

MacGilchrist, I. (2010), *The Master and his Emissary: The Divided Brain and the Making of the Western World*. London: Yale University Press.

National Advisory Committee on Creative and Cultural Education (NACCCE) (1999), *All Our Futures: Creativity, Culture and Education*. London: DfEE.

Pinker, S. (2003), *The Blank Slate: The Modern Denial of Human Nature*. London: Penguin.

Sousa, D., Ansari, D. and Christodoulou, J. (2010), *Mind, Brain, & Education: Neuroscience Implications for the Classroom*. Bloomington, IL: Solution Tree Press.

Vygotsky, L. (1978), *Mind in Society: The Development of Higher Psychological Processes*. Cambridge, MA: Harvard University Press.

Do schools need to promote SMSC to ensure children have a quality learning experience?

Rosemary Walters

2

What is spiritual, moral, social and cultural development (SMSC)? If we don't know what it is how can we promote it? Isn't it just Religious Education (RE) anyway? A summary of the definitions of SMSC and the implications for school life might look like this:

Spiritual: *Self Awareness and Finding Meaning*
Moral: *Action, Understanding Right, Wrong and Consequences*
Social: *Interaction, Positive Relationship and Participation*
Cultural: *Belonging and Celebrating Diversity.* (from Eaude 2006)

The Office for Standards in Education (OfSTED) 2014 Supplementary Inspection Guidance (for England) provides this short introduction which is followed by a fuller definition of each of the four elements:

> When considering how well the school promotes pupils' SMSC, inspectors should take into account the impact of the range of opportunities provided for them to develop their self-esteem and confidence. (OfSTED 2014: 37)

This raises the question:

What do you understand by the concepts 'spiritual', 'moral', 'social' and 'cultural' in a school environment? Are the above definitions useful or accurate?

The SMSC agenda in England is not one of standards to be reached by everyone in the same way and to an approved and measured level. How can it be if it is to include the intangible? To grow up in these contexts implies that opportunities are given primarily to reflect on beliefs, values and learning experiences. This can be done through stopping and wondering at the mysteries and curiosities which emerge from children learning new things about themselves and the world.

What would be evidence of development for each of the concepts? If SMSC is not to be measured against set targets is it meaningful to link it with learning at all?

For example, the word 'spiritual' has roots in the Latin 'spirare', to breathe and it implies an animation, a giving of life to an individual or a community. This raises a key question of whether spirituality has to be religious. Can this animation and the consequent creativity be present in all communities of learning or is it the special prerogative of faith-based schools? What sort of life will be given and received? The fact that OfSTED in England are requiring all school inspections to include judgements on 'the range of opportunities provided for them (the pupils) to develop their self-esteem and confidence' (OfSTED 2014: 37) implies a very broad and secular definition but does not exclude the influence of faith in this development.

Can spiritual development be inclusive or do you see it as essentially 'religious'? Can/should schools foster spirituality? Is it innate in everyone?

The key to providing a range of such opportunities is partly that of giving time for reflection throughout the curriculum to ponder on mystery. All subject areas have the potential to provide time for investigating, wondering and marvelling; exploring and responding; looking, listening and creating; finding patterns and discovering and expressing and articulating the joy of learning.

Choose two subject areas of the primary curriculum. How could you plan for the children to experience and identify the types of reflection described above? What opportunities might there be to plan specifically for cultural development within these?

The chance for children to identify these moments is part of the enchantment of childhood in a world of materialism, competition and consumerism into which society and culture are only too keen to initiate them. In neglecting this enchantment, the dimensions of spiritual intelligence, that is the capacity to experience self-awareness and awe and wonder, and the dimensions of emotional intelligence, that is the capacity to value one's self and others, are often forgotten to the detriment of deep learning.

SMSC is beyond being the sole brief of RE, although in RE there will be specific chances to encounter the spirituality of a variety of religions as they respond to ultimate questions, engaging with the mysteries of creation, suffering and ultimate meaning. Reflecting on beliefs and values from the past, the present and for the future can occur in Art, Geography, History, and Science and can stimulate discussion on the reasoning behind moral values which will implicitly include discussion on the social development of positive relationships. Expanding the child's horizon from a secure sense of belonging and identity allows them to celebrate their own place in the world and in culturally diverse situations rather than being threatened by them.

Saljo (1979) has five conceptions of learning and delineates numbers four and five as 'deep'. These two are; 'learning as making sense or abstracting meaning', this learning involves relating parts of the subject matter to each other and to the real world; 'learning as interpreting and understanding reality in a different way', this learning involves comprehending the world by reinterpreting knowledge. Deep learning can take place only when the child is engaged in a self-affirming positive personal relationship with the exploration of the subject matter and in the course of this with other learners. It is important that teachers ensure that the atmosphere in their class is conducive to such learning. Deep learning is characterized by inspiration firing the motivation of authentic curiosity and the application of that learning to the practical application of issues arising from living in a learning community.

Can you justify how you might relate Saljo's deep learning conceptions of making sense, relating to the real world and understanding reality differently to each of the elements of SMSC?

The atmosphere around the school is a crucial reflection of how far SMSC principles are being identified and encouraged. Displays, notices, library books and resources and the whole air of tidiness, courtesy and purposeful, challenging collaborative activity around the school alongside a wide variety of extracurricular activities will produce evidence of SMSC. Appreciating the joy and value of knowledge in the widest sense of reflecting on human responses to ultimate questions, on human successes and failures, on how to define and live moral lives and on building functioning and inclusive communities while celebrating diversity, should be expressed in the daily routine and life of the school and they should be apparent to a visitor as soon as they step into the school environment.

A recent report on SMSC from the RSA Action and Research Centre has the significant title, *Schools with Soul* (Peterson et al. 2014). Key findings (pp. 16–21) include:

- the danger of SMSC getting marginalized
- the need to explore the concepts of spirituality and well-being
- the lack of incentive and time for schools to reflect on long-term purpose, aims and ethos

- the lack of coherent vision, planning and delivery for SMSC
- the 'sanitisation' of SMSC as teachers fear the encounter with relevant and possibly controversial issues with their pupils.

How would you illustrate what is meant by the 'soul' of a school using these findings if you were a head teacher?

SMSC has the potential to contribute the three Es' to the primary curriculum, 'enriching', 'enlarging' and 'enhancing' the learning experience of the children. These complementary perspectives can offer curriculum balance at a time when there is a tendency towards surface learning from a standards driven, strictly measurable agenda, all too often based for the children on the fear of official definitions of failure. SMSC holds to the vision that the spirit gives life and acknowledges that there is an element of mystery in the subject and in the teaching and learning (Webster 2010). Gent (2002) suggests that there is a direct link between teachers' spirituality and teacher retention. If it is planned, monitored and embedded with conviction in the ethos and life of the school, this link might work towards a positive outcome for the lives of individual teachers and therefore the retention of creative and enthusiastic newly qualified teachers.

Why do you think Gent expresses this opinion? What are the reasons for your answer?

References and further reading

Best, R. (ed.) (1996), *Education, Spirituality and the Whole Child.* London: Cassell.

Best, R. (2000), *Education for Spiritual, Moral and Social Development.* London: Continuum.

Bigger, S. and Brown, E. (eds) (1999), *Spiritual, Moral, Social and Cultural Education.* London: Fulton.

Citizenship Foundation (2014), www.doingsmsc.org.uk (accessed February 2014).

Copley, T. (2000), *Spiritual Development in the State School.* Exeter: University of Exeter.

Erricker, C. and Erricker, J. (2000), *Reconstructing Religious, Spiritual and Moral Education.* London: Routledge Falmer.

Eaude, T. (2006), *Children's Spiritual, Moral, Social and Cultural Development.* Exeter: Learning Matters.

Gent, B. (Spring 2002), 'Spiritual Development and School Life: Finding the words', *Resource,* 24, (2), www.pcfre.org.uk (accessed March 2014).

Grey, M. (April 2006), 'The disenchantment and re-enchantment of childhood in an age of globalisation', *International Journal of Children's Spirituality,* 11, (1), 11–21.

Hull, J. (Summer 2002), 'Spiritual Development: Interpretations and Applications', *British Journal of Religious Education,* 24, (3), 171–82.

Office for Standards in Education (OfSTED) (2014), *Subsidiary Guidance Supporting the Inspection of Maintained Schools and Academies*, www.ofsted.gov.uk (accessed February 2014).

Peterson, A., Lexmond, J., Hallgarten, J. and Kerr, D. (2014), *Schools with Soul: A New Approach to Spiritual, Moral, Social and Cultural Education* RSA Action and Research Centre, www.thersa.org/smsc (accessed March 2014).

Saljo, R. (1979), *Learning in the Learner's Perspective: 1: Some Commonplace Conceptions* (Report No. 76). Gothenburg, Sweden: University of Gothenburg, Institute of Education, http://www.learningandteaching.info/learning/deepsurf.htm (accessed February 2014).

Webster, M. (2010), *Creative Approaches to Teaching Primary RE*. London: Longman.

3 'He's one of yours'. Does the belief in a specialist pedagogy for children with a special educational need disempower teachers?

Andy Bloor

This is a tempting scenario: there is a child in your class with whom you are struggling. It may be that they have a learning difficulty and this means that they are consistently falling behind their peers. It may be that they have a behavioural or mental health difficulty and this means they are unable to access the curriculum in the normal sense. Whatever the root cause they are in your class and are not making any progress. Then you realize they have an identified Special Educational Need (SEN)[1] and you breathe a sigh of relief. You have had educational absolution; they are 'one of those'; a child who comes under the auspices of the specialist in your school: the Special Needs Coordinator (SENCo).

But there is another angle. You are the SENCo. A young, possibly inexperienced teacher comes to you. There is a child in their class and they have been identified as 'one of yours'. The teacher is looking at you for hope; absolution from either responsibility or blame for the apparent lack of progress that this child is making in their class.

This is a scenario I come across all too often in our schools. And after all, who can blame a teacher in this position? With a class of 30 children it is tempting to block them into groups for ease of planning and expectation; a variation on higher ability/middle ability/lower ability is the most common. But what about children who lie beyond these categories? If they have a diagnosis, what can you do to support them? What if you make no difference or, even worse, cause them harm? Surely that's a real danger if a child has a medical diagnosis?

There are no hard and fast rules but one thing is clear: just as a doctor has a duty to 'treat the patient in front of him' so we as teachers have a duty – one which can never be absolved – to teach the child in front of us. And yet, the lingering doubt remains; what can I as a general primary school teacher do to teach a child with a specialist diagnosis?

What kind of support do you think you can expect?

The Warnock Report (HMSO 1978) noted that whatever the root cause of a child's difficulty in school, be it familial or social, unless support was forthcoming that helped that child, then they would fall behind in their education, through an experience of prolonged failure.

Can you think of a time when you were a child where you needed extra support in the classroom?

The inference here is that SEN goes beyond a diagnosis; that SEN is more than a pervasive medical condition. Norwich and Lewis (2007) note that while many teachers believe that Special Education means Special Teaching, there is little evidence to support this position. This belief is often referred to as the Specialist Pedagogy approach. It is what leads to the scenario we looked at in the opening paragraphs of this chapter.

Can you think of an occasion where your teaching methods were substantially different for a child with a SEN than any other child in the class?

Hiebert et al. (2002, cited in Black-Hawkins and Florian 2012) note that, ' we were keen to 'recognize the potential of [teachers'] personal knowledge as it becomes transformed into professional knowledge' (p. 572).

Imagine now a different scenario from the one at the start of this chapter. A teacher sees a child in their class who is struggling to maintain their attention in the class. The teacher notes that the child's attention is worse in Literacy when they are seated near the window at the back of the class. The teacher tries sitting the child nearer the front (closer to her) and away from the window. The child shows greater concentration in Literacy lessons.

Two months later the child receives a diagnosis of ADHD. How should the teacher's response change?

It could easily be argued that it shouldn't change at all. The teacher successfully identified a difficulty the child had and tried a change of approach. This approach was beneficial to the child's learning progress through increased attention. If the teacher had subscribed to a 'specialist pedagogy' approach, then they would have felt disempowered by a medical diagnosis. In this new approach, instead of seeing it as a potential destabilizing of the work already undertaken, the teacher sees it as an opportunity to draw on those who have worked in this field to augment their own approaches.

We all need to know our boundaries when supporting a child with a Special Educational Need – *what* we can and cannot do on our own and *when* to draw on specialist support. This should mean that we feel empowered to support the children in our class and maintain ownership of their education. A 'specialist pedagogy' does not mean we do not need specialist support; but it does mean that when we have what Hiebert et al. (2002) referred to as the personal knowledge transformed into the professional, we do not allow ourselves to become disempowered by a label from those outside our classroom.

Note

1 Special Educational Needs (SEN) is a legally recognized term in England and Wales that describes a child requiring additional support to attain their potential in school.

References and further reading

Black-Hawkins, K. and Florian, L. (2012), 'Classroom teachers' craft knowledge of their inclusive practice', *Teachers and Teaching: Theory and Practice*, 18, (5), 567–84.

Her Majesty's Stationary Office (HMSO) (1978), *Report of the Committee of Enquiry into the Education of Handicapped Children and Young People* (The Warnock Report), http://www.educationengland. org.uk/documents/warnock/warnock1978.html (accessed March 2014).

Hiebert, J., Gallimore, R. and Stigler, J. (2002), 'A knowledge base for the teaching profession: What would it look like and how can we get one?', *Educational Researcher*, 31, (5), 3–15.

Norwich, B. and Lewis, A. (2007), 'How specialized is teaching children with disabilities and difficulties?', *Journal of Curriculum Studies*, 39, (2), 127–50.

Why can't children play in reception?

Karen Vincent

4

> All they have done this year in reception is play. I can't wait until they go into year 1 [5-6 year-olds], then they can start to learn.

This statement is indicative of some of the comments that I have heard both as a parent of two reception-aged children and as a teacher of reception-aged and year one children. This view could be said to be based upon a fundamental opinion that children 'become ready' to learn and that play has little to do with the serious business of real learning.

At what point do you think children are ready to learn and what role do you think play has in children's learning?

Gopnik, Melzoff and Kuhl (1999: 1) remind us that we are born with the capacity to learn, 'what we see in the crib is the greatest mind that has ever existed, the most powerful learning machine in the universe'. By the time children come to school, they have already learnt a phenomenal amount, largely through imitation and exploration with a bit of being told and having to listen or be shown. They are accomplished learners.

I want to give you the opportunity to reflect upon 'play' and how it is a powerful motivator for learning in the reception years and beyond. It is an essential part of the process of learning and should not be seen as something that is separate and different. Consider your own views of play:

Do you see it as something that only children in the early years or reception year (0–5-year-olds) should be allowed to do?

Do you think that KS1 (5–7-year-olds) should incorporate more play-based approaches?

Do you see any benefit in enabling children in KS2 (7–11–year-olds) to play?

Do you consider play to be inseparable and unremittingly infused with learning, that is, play is learning and learning is play or do you see it as a means to an end such as a way of occupying children until you can spend some 'quality teacher time' with them?

Moyles (1989) highlights some of the difficulties with defining play. It is a complex and highly contentious area of education. There are many differing views and each reader will hold their own theories and perceptions in mind. There is no doubt, however, that for young children, play is integrated with their learning experiences. Play is essentially an exploration of a process or an object. The 'player' is attempting to fit the new knowledge into their existing mental framework. Piaget's theories about assimilation and accommodation offer us a way of understanding this process (1978). Think about how you learn about how to use a new laptop or piece of equipment. Do you studiously read through the instruction manual before you open the lid and follow the instructions? I suspect not. Most of us would begin exploring by turning it on and using our existing knowledge to construct understandings of how this new equipment works. Likewise, play gives children the opportunity to 'play out' their internal thought processes physically. It allows them to create and influence the process and ultimately the product at the end. Deep intrinsic desire drives the action and an environment that supports the learning of new skills and ideas will nurture early learning dispositions. Think about how you respond to tasks. If you are told how to do something and asked to replicate it, your motivation will possibly not be as high as doing a task that you have initiated yourself, based upon a real and driving curiosity to find out more about something.

David (1999), states that activities which stem from the child's interests, and therefore produce intrinsic motivation, are more likely to lead to effective learning. Early learning dispositions need nurturing in order to allow young children to develop flexibility of thought, understand symbolic representation and foster persistence and success. These are all key aspects of being a learner. Young children do not own play, but they play more because more in the world is new to them. And this, combined with their innate curiosity, means that they naturally seem to be open to new experiences.

Consider how you initiate tasks for children to develop. Are they tasks to be done for the teacher or are they territories to be explored? How might young children respond to these tasks as a consequence? Give some examples from your practice.

Nurturing and enhancing young children's learning dispositions are fundamental in creating powerful and competent learners, and this, combined with a vibrant and interesting environment that fosters curiosity will enable children to learn about the world around them. Wood and Attfield (2005) call these attitudes and dispositions, 'can-do orientations' and they draw attention to the presence of curiosity and interest as well as willingness to take risks and show resilience, enthusiasm and self-efficacy.

For many young children, movement is bound up with physical, intellectual and emotional development. Movement can be an important facet of learning how to represent our thoughts and feelings. For example, two girls are encouraging each other to climb to the top of the wooden climbing frame. They are supporting each other emotionally as they offer advice to put their 'foot on that step' or 'hold on to that piece of rope' as one swings it towards the other. As each child climbs, they are regulating their fear, finding new ways of climbing and exploring the limits of their body's capability. This is supported by their encouragement and motivation towards each other. They begin to understand a new view of the world from a higher perspective as they work together. Some teachers may consider this as an unwelcome risk or even dangerous behaviour and attempt to prevent an accident by standing very close or instructing them to 'come down'. But let us consider what learning is taking place. They are clearly motivated by the activity and are demonstrating high levels of well-being and involvement. They are working at the limits of their body's capability, trying out and taking new risks. We can see that this activity contains examples of early Science and Maths as they estimate and experience distance and height as they climb and as they estimate the angle of the rope as it swings between them. They are problem solving as well as exploring. They are also socializing and empathizing with each other. The teacher's role here is to provide extended opportunities and to observe and reflect on the impact of these in order to identify the learning and provide further opportunities to extend it.

How could this 'play' activity be extended and what is its potential for learning?

Understanding the value of play within your classroom will enable you to engage with empowered and motivated children who enjoy and feel safe to take risks in new, previously unexplored territories. Ultimately, learning is about knowing something that you didn't know before. By taking account of how young children learn, you will be opening up new avenues of learning for them. Having a clear view of what play and learning means to you will enable you to provide worthwhile and meaningful experiences for the children in your class.

References and further reading

Bilton, H. (2010), *Outdoor Learning in the Early Years*. London: David Fulton.

Blakemore, S. and Frith, U. (2005), *The Learning Brain*. Oxford: Blackwell.

Broadhead, P., Howard, J. and Wood, E. (2010), *Play and Learning in the Early Years*. London: Sage.

David, T. (1999), *Young Children Learning*. London: Sage.

Gopnik, A., Melzoff, A. and Kuhl, P. (1999), *How Babies Think*. London: Phoenix.

Meadows, S. (1993), *The Child as Thinker*. London: Routledge.

Moyles, J. (1989), *Just Playing?* Berkshire: Oxford University Press.

—(2010), *Thinking about Play*. Berkshire: McGraw Hill.

Piaget, J. (1978), *The Development of Thought: Equilibration of Cognitive Structures*. Oxford: Blackwell cited by Meadows, S. (1993), *The Child as Thinker*. London: Routledge.

For more on Piaget's theories read: Donaldson, M. (1978), *Children's Minds*. London: Fontana or, Garhart Mooney, C. (2000), *Theories of Childhood*. USA: Redleaf.

Tovey, H. (2007), *Playing Outdoors: Spaces and Places, Risk and Challenge*. Berkshire: Oxford University Press.

Wood, E. and Attfield, J. (2005), *Play, Learning and the Early Childhood Curriculum*. London: Paul Chapman.

Is learning through practical work worth the effort?

Gill Hope

5

The short answer to this question is, 'Undoubtedly, yes'. All forms of hands-on experiential learning are more likely to be remembered than listening and recording (Harrison 1978). The longer answer is as follows: It depends on what kind of practical activity the children are doing. It is not sufficient to be making something in which the only choices children have are the pattern or the colour. An example of such limitation is the making of 'Egyptian cuffs' which are strips of paper that go around the wrists decorated with hieroglyphs. No thinking skills are required. It is just a low-level drawing and colouring exercise.

However, when children have the opportunity to engage in designing through making, they can see their own ideas come to fruition and see themselves as active agents in the creation of new things. By learning through making an object of their own imagination, children can turn an idea that exists in their mind's eye into something real and tangible. In Parkinson's research into young children's practical design-and-make activity (2012), he identified the skills of making, manipulating, modelling, mending and modifying which he called the '5 Ms'. These are not simply physical skills, but relate directly to the development of cognitive capacities. As children manipulate the parts of the objects they are making, the visual image in their mind's eye is being rotated and modified through constantly re-imaging the ideas within their brains (Roberts 1992).

As you observe children designing and making how many of Parkinson's '5 Ms' can you observe in the course of 5 minutes?

At the heart of the new National Curriculum for Design and Technology (DfE 2014) is the firmly held belief that children need to undertake real tasks with real materials and components that allow them to model and create real technological solutions. In Design and Technology there is more to the teaching and learning than just setting up practical activities. The outcome must be a functional product with a specific user and purpose in mind (or a model of one; children's work is often in paper and card). My own research (Hope 2002) into children's use of drawing for designing showed that as children were constructing a product in their imagination, they were manipulating their inner images and trying to get them down on paper; they were modifying their ideas in discussion with friends; amending ideas as new ones came to light; modelling ideas in their mind and expressing them in talk, pictures and written words. They even did this with each other's ideas, 'What you could do is'. The products they then made were both imaginative and functional.

The National Curriculum for Design and Technology (DfE 2014) in England is very specific about the process skills within the subject: designing, making and evaluating. Although these skills have of necessity been separated out in order to elucidate what they mean, the deliberate choice of the word iterative in the paragraphs that head the programmes of study for both Key Stages 1 and 2 is intended to indicate strongly to teachers that designing is not a linear process. This is not 'designing' separated from 'making' separated from 'evaluating'. All three skills are inter-related and occur cyclically within the whole of the production process from first ideas to standing back and admiring the finished product.

A key word in the new NC in both KS1 and 2 is 'iterative' – What does this word mean in the context of the 3 core NC skills (designing, making, evaluating)?

As soon as a new project is introduced to the class, ideas are generated in the children's mind and begin to be evaluated. It may be that one strong good idea comes to mind that just needs some tweaking and modification, or maybe a whole series of possibilities can be seen. Some quick sketches might help to clarify ideas at this stage but the ideas that go forward, half-formed in the child's head, will need real materials that can be manipulated so that they think through the making, modifying and mending as they begin to model their ideas in the physical form (Parkinson 2012).

The dual metaphor at the heart of my own research was design as both a 'container' and a 'journey' (Hope 2006). A drawing may contain some initial ideas but it is only as part of a design journey that it has any sense of purpose. Initial ideas might equally well be contained in a model made with a construction kit, a list of ideas discussed with friends, an annotated recipe downloaded from the internet or photographs taken on a visit to a local playground. An audio recording of a group design discussion could be played to another group who then jot down their responses to feed back to the originators. Mock-ups can be made from cheap or free resources to be evaluated before cutting into more expensive ones.

As you plan design and technology lessons, how will you ensure children are able to make genuine design decisions throughout the lesson or throughout a sequence of lessons?

I have focused my discussion on design and technology because this is the subject in the curriculum where the benefits of practical work are most clearly laid out. There is no reason why these skills should not also be encouraged and developed within other subjects or in cross-curricular work. Many topics provide rich contexts for deep creative thinking. For instance, the new National Curriculum for Design and Technology (DfE 2014) for England makes explicit reference to the history of technology. Therefore, when studying the Tudors one might imagine being one of Walter Raleigh's colonists: What kind of house would they build? Where will they keep the cow? What ideas about houses did the people take with them to Virginia? Can the children design and build a model of a suitable house for a colonist? This level of thinking requires deep engagement with the experience of the people of the time and an appreciation of the realities of how they lived.

Davies et al. (2001) assert that there exist strong links between practical designing-and-making and core intra-personal and inter-personal skills, including spirituality and citizenship. Through designing their own solutions to technological problems, children develop their creative and logical problem-solving skills; their ability to apply knowledge from other areas of life and the curriculum; to think about the needs and wants of others; to imagine the future and to see themselves and others as being capable agents in its creation, development and sustainability. The sense of achievement and pride in their finished product coupled to the ability to appreciate and praise the achievements of each other, is the same, say Davies et al. (2001) as the sense of awe and wonder at the greatest achievements of humankind, whether this be the Pyramids or the Shard; the cave paintings of Altamira or the mosaics of Ravenna; a stone axe discovered in the gravel beds at Happisburgh or the iPhone that they hold in their hand today.

Is practical work worth the effort?

Can we inspire children to think great thoughts and take home something to be proud of and say 'I made that'; to value the help of their friends; to be part of a team that solved the problem, to win the robot car race, or to believe in their own efficacy to make, mend, fix, create and design the future?

References and further reading

Davies, D., Howe, A. and Ritchie, R. (2001), *Primary Design & Technology for the Future: Creativity, Culture & Citizenship*. London: David Fulton Publishers.

Department for Education (DfE) (2014), *National Curriculum for Design and Technology*. London: Department for Education.

Harrison, A. (1978), *Making & Thinking*. London: The Harvester Press.

Hope, G. (2002), *Drawing as a Tool for Thought*, (unpublished Ph.D. thesis) University of London.

—(2006), *Teaching Design and Technology in Key Stages 1 and 2*. Exeter: Learning Matters.

Parkinson, E. F. (2012) (unpublished PhD thesis) Construction Kits and Technological Literacy; Canterbury Christ Church University.

Roberts, P. (1992), 'Of models, modelling & design: An applied philosophical enquiry in modelling: The language of design', *Design Occasional Papers No 1*, Department of Design and Technology, Loughborough University of Technology.

What do teachers gain from organizing educational visits?

Michael Green

6

Despite the wealth of literature and research identifying the countless benefits of children being provided with a diverse range of opportunities to learn outside the classroom (Gould 2003; Dillon et al. 2006; Peacock 2006; Malone 2008; Ofsted 2008; DfES 2006), there is a growing body of research which considers the notion of a school trip from the perspective the challenges present to the teachers themselves. The centrality of teachers in determining the success and impact of school trips on children is unquestioned (Waite 2009). There is, therefore, a strong case to argue that in order for teachers to have a positive influence, they too need to see themselves as learners while on a school trip and consider the learning opportunities that school trips can offer to their personal and professional development.

If we are going to consider whether teachers can view school trips as a learning opportunity for themselves, we need to understand their views and opinions about school trips in general as this may have a significant influence and may also go some way to explain some teachers' behaviours while on a school trip. Generally two challenges emerge, 'health and safety' and 'confidence'.

In a survey of geography teachers (Parry and Clarke 2004) 62 per cent of those questioned either agreed or strongly agreed that they were deterred from organizing field trips because of the threat of legal action should anything go wrong. Research by the National Foundation for Educational Research (NfER 2006) echoes this, highlighting teachers' concerns over health and safety and the possibility of litigation. Waite (2009) goes so far as to question whether the issue of child safety has gone too far in schools and is now acting as a barrier to children's learning and development. Hackitt (2007), the Chair of the Health and Safety Commission, argues that the issue of health and safety and threats of litigation has been considerably distorted which has created a culture of fear in education. This view is reinforced by the government (DCSF 2009) when they issued a statement stating that 'schools should not let ungrounded fears of a compensation culture deny children educational opportunities'. OfSTED (2008: 42) reported that 'poor behaviour; logistical difficulties, including the large numbers of pupils involved; disruption to the timetable; cost; health and safety issues and cultural barriers' were cited by senior leaders as challenges to engaging in geography fieldwork in schools.

In your experience, is this true in primary schools?

Barker et al. (2002) and Rickinson et al. (2004) attribute a decline in the number of school trips to the 'fear factor'. While fears over litigation certainly appeared to be a key factor in teachers' perspectives regarding school trips, the research identifies an underlying issue relating to a lack of teacher confidence in relation to organizing school trips (NfER 2006). OfSTED's research in 2004 concerning good practice in outdoor learning identified a direct link between teachers who lacked confidence in school trips and the lack of quality opportunities then afforded to children to learn outside the classroom.

I would argue that teachers need to consider and reflect upon the opportunities for their own learning and development as a result of their engagement in the school trip. Such reflection has the potential to act as a catalyst for improvement to practice, which in turn, will benefit their pupils and possibly increase the number of trips undertaken.

Would recognition of personal and professional benefit counterbalance the time and effort required to organize trips?

Roberts, in his report on *Nurturing Creativity in Young People* argued strongly that such opportunities are essential if we are to get teachers to 'think about alternative approaches to teaching and learning' (Roberts 2006: 47) and Anderson et al. (2006) make a direct link between teacher opportunity and the impact it will have on children's experiences; 'First-hand experience during teacher training or the early years of teaching seems likely to influence fieldtrip practice' (p. 380). Darling-Hammond (1997) suggests that 'teachers learn just as their students do' (ibid., 1997: 319); therefore, it does not seem unreasonable to consider that a teacher might enjoy a school trip as much as his or her pupils, even viewing it entirely as a learning experience for themselves. The research of Dillon et al. (2006) has identified several areas of learning for teachers through their participation in school trips, here summarized:

Having the opportunity to observe the expertise of others
Developing different styles of teaching
Acquiring new subject knowledge that could be applied in their own classrooms
Having the opportunity to learn more about their pupils in a relatively relaxed, informal environment

What is your own experience of learning in relation to a school trip?

Parallels here can be drawn to Sangster and Green's research (2010) focusing on the learning opportunities for student teachers to experience learning outside the classroom. According to Hanna's research (1992) much of this 'reluctance' can be attributed to a lack of in-service and pre-service training opportunities being provided to teachers to develop the skills and confidence to effectively use learning opportunities beyond the classroom. Dillon et al. (2005) concur and stress that there is a 'need' for teachers to have a better understanding of how children learn outside the classroom. The 2010 Government Select Committee Report made the case that professional development in relation to learning outside the classroom is pivotal;

> Teachers need to be exposed to learning outside the curriculum from early on in their career, and this should not be left to chance. We expect to see a clearer and more consistent presence for learning outside the classroom across initial teacher training and early career and ongoing professional development for teachers. (Children, Schools and Families Committee, DCSF 2010: 7)

Are there are sufficient opportunities being offered for in-service teachers to receive CPD training in school trips?

Recent research has identified a need for specific school trip pedagogy to be considered more strongly (Kisiel 2005). Rea et al. (2009) argue that learning outdoors on school trips is considerably different to learning in class and should not be viewed as an extension of what happens inside schools.

The literature seems to indicate that the key characteristics of professional development involve reflection, analysis and inquiry in order to develop one's beliefs and ideas which has the potential to bring about change in one's classroom practice (Kolb 1984; Austin 2007; Keiny, 1994; Pollard 2002). To what extent though does this opportunity arise before, during and after a school trip? Anderson et al. (2006) point out that the success of a school trip is dependent on the influence of the teacher, and therefore opportunities for development are pivotal. If we also want teachers to learn as well from the experience, time and space need to be created for critical refection to take place. Dewey (1933) placed considerable emphasis on the importance of having the opportunity to critically reflect on the experience. He (1933: 9) warns that 'experience alone is not sufficient for learning to occur'. This has significant implications for teachers in terms of viewing school trips as an opportunity for their own learning if there is no time for reflection.

Emerging from the discussion is certainly the notion that school trips may be an untapped opportunity for teachers to engage in reflection not only on teaching and learning, but also on gaining their own personal and professional development. One issue though that causes me much consternation is the extent to which space and opportunity is provided for such reflection to take place.

References and further reading

Anderson, D., Kisiel, J. and Storksdiek, M. (2006), 'Understanding Teachers' Perspectives on Fieldtrips: Discovering common ground in three countries', *Curator*, 49, (3), 365–86.

Austin, R. (ed.) (2007), *Letting the Outside in: Developing Teaching and Learning Beyond the Early Years Classroom*. Stoke-on-Trent: Trentham Books.

Barker, S., Slingsby, D. and Tilling, S. (2002), *Teaching Biology Outside the Classroom: Is it Heading for Extinction? A Report on Biology Fieldwork in the 14-19 Curriculum*. Shrewsbury: Field Studies Council.

Beames, S., Higgins, P. and Nicol, R. (2012), *Learning Outside the Classroom: Theory and Guidelines for Practice*. London: Routledge.

Curtis, P. (2009), 'Children denied school trips over teachers' fears of being sued', http://www.theguardian.com/education/2009/oct/02/school-trips-teachers-legal-action (accessed March 2011).

Darling-Hammond, L. (1997), *The Right to Learn: A Blueprint for Creating Schools that Work*. San Francisco: Jossey Bass.

Department for Children, Schools and Families (2009), 'Children denied school trips over teachers' fears of being sued', in P. Curtis (ed.), http://www.theguardian.com/education/2009/oct/02/school-trips-teachers-legal-action (accessed March 2011).

—(2010), *Transforming Education Outside the Classroom: Responses from the Government and Ofsted to the Sixth Report of the Children, Schools and Families Committee, Session 2009-10*. London: The Stationery Office Ltd.

Department for Education and Skills (2006), *Learning Outside the Classroom Manifesto*. London: DfES.

Dewey, J. (1933), *How We Think: A Restatement of the Relation of Reflective Thinking to the Educative Process*. Lexington, MA: DC Heath and Company.

Dillon, J., Morris, M., O'Donnell, L., Rickinson, M. and Scott, W. (2005), *Engaging and Learning with the Outdoors*. Bath: Centre for Research in Environmental Education.

Dillon, J., Rickinson, M., Teamey, K., Morris, M., Choi, M., Sanders, D. and Benefield, P. (2006), 'The value of outdoor learning: Evidence from research in the UK and elsewhere', *School Science* Review, 87, 107–11.

Gould, H. (2003), *Settings Other than Schools: Initial Teacher Training Placements in Museums, Libraries and Archives*. Yorkshire: YMLAC.

Hackitt, J. 'Learning to Manage Risk - Part of Growing Up', A Health and Safety Executive press release, 1 November 2007, http://news.hse.gov.uk/2007/11/01/learning-to-manage-risks-part-of-growing-up/ (accessed July 2014).

Hanna, G. (1992), 'Jumping Deadfall: Overcoming barriers to implementing outdoor and environmental education', Paper presented at the International Conference for the *Association of Experiential Education*, 8–11 October, Alberta Canada. http://www.eric.ed.gov/ERICWebPortal/custom/portlets/recordDetails/detailmini.jsp?_nfpb=true&_&ERICExtSearch_SearchValue_0=ED353112&ERICExtSearch_SearchType_0=no&accno=ED353112 (accessed September 2010).

Keiny, S. (1994), 'Constructivism and teachers' professional development', *Teaching and Teacher Education*, 10, (2), 157–67.

Kisiel, J. (2005), 'Understanding Elementary Teacher Motivations for Science Fieldtrips', *Science Education*, 89, (6), 936–55.

Kolb, D. (1984), *Experiential Learning: Experience as the Source of Learning and Development*. New Jersey: Prentice-Hall.

Malone, K. (2008), *Every Experience Matters*. Stoneleigh: Farming and Countryside Education.

NfER (2006), *Education Outside the Classroom: Research to Identify What Training is Offered by Initial Teacher Training Institutions*. London: DfES.

OfSTED (2004), *Outdoor Education: Aspects of Good Practice*. London: OfSTED.

—(2008), *Learning Outside the Classroom: How Far Should You Go?* London: OfSTED.

Parry, G. and Clarke, L. (2004), 'Risk Assessment and Geography Teachers: A survey', *Education and the Law*, 16, (2–3), 115–31.

Peacock, A. (2006), *Changing Minds: The Lasting Impact of School Trips*. Exeter: University of Exeter.

Pollard, A. (ed.) (2002), *Readings for Reflective Teaching*. London: Continuum.

Rea, T. and Waite, S. (2009), 'International Perspectives on outdoor and experiential learning', *Education 3-13*, 37, (1), 1–4.

Rickinson, M., Dillon, J., Teamey, K., Morris, M., Choi, M., Sanders, D. and Benefield, P. (2004), *A Review of Research on Outdoor Learning*. Shrewsbury: Field Studies Council.

Roberts, P. (2006), *Nurturing Creativity in Young People: A Report to Government to Inform Policy*. London: DCMS.

Sangster, M. and Green. M. (2010), 'The Value of an Alternative Placement for Student Teachers in Initial Teacher Education', Paper presented at the *European Education Research Conference*, Helsinki, 25–27 September, http://www.eera-ecer.eu/ecer-programmes/conference/ecer-2010/contribution/730-2/?no_cache=1&cHash=21044039e2 (accessed October 2010).

Waite, S. (2009) 'Outdoor Learning for children aged 2-11: perceived barriers, potential solutions', *Conference Proceedings for International Outdoor Education Research Conference*, La Trobe University, Beechworth, Australia, 15–18 April 2009, www.latrobe.edu.au/education/assets/downloads/2009-conference-waite.pdf (accessed March 2011).

—(2011), *Children Learning Outside the Classroom from Birth to Eleven*. London: Sage.

7

How do classroom dynamics affect learning?

Mark Hardman

We start each lesson with a learning objective and then, through carefully matching activities to that objective, the pupils learn what we intended them to. 'It's simple isn't it?' Perhaps it is a bit too simple. In this chapter, I am going to argue that learning is 'non-linear' and that our classrooms are complex places. I am also going to argue that this should not be a source of worry because we already know how to deal with the complexities of learning.

The view of learning as a very 'linear' process, with the input of an activity leading to the output of learning, can be attributed to The National Strategies which ran in England between 1997 and 2011. The focus on clear objectives and assessment against these had a positive impact on the attainment of pupils (DfE 2011). However, there is a feeling that sometimes teachers are 'playing a game', whereby they are able to show that pupils meet the objectives, but they are not fully convinced that learning has taken place. Experienced teachers see this when the pupils have completely forgotten what they 'learned' yesterday, but I also see it when new teachers first look at assessment in classrooms. Like the child in *The Emperor's New Clothes*, a minority of new teachers see that it is not really learning that is being measured but a pupil's ability to say the right thing. The difficulty of actually measuring learning is that we don't really understand what it is.

What is learning? How do you know when you see it?

Attainment is the performance of a child on a test or in a task but learning is much messier. Although educational neuroscience is way too young for us to draw any firm conclusions, there is growing evidence that the brain might be seen as a 'non-linear' or 'complex' system. Computer models (Cilliers 1998), experimental work (Freeman 1999) and cognitive neuroscience (Kelso 1995) all suggest that when we learn, there is a change in the pattern of electrical signals across the brain. However, this does not happen in a simple way; the new brain pattern suddenly emerges and there is an abrupt change in brain function. This will not be surprising to teachers, who talk about 'light bulb moments' when pupils suddenly 'get it'.

Furthermore, there is whole body of evidence that pupils' ideas are often resistant to teaching (Brown and Hammer 2008); that is, they continue to hold naïve views despite a huge effort on the part of the teacher. Then, a seemingly inconsequential influence makes them suddenly shift their thinking. This is what I mean by 'non-linear'; there is not a simple relationship between what is taught and the influence it has. Viewing learning in this way seems to fit the tacit experience of teachers better than seeing learning as a simple input–outcome process. Learning is highly sensitive to the history of the learner and the context at any moment in time. But if learning is sensitive to the context in which pupils learn, then that means our classrooms have an influence on how pupils learn.

Do different classes 'feel' different; is there a 'class dynamic'?

Learning comes about by pupils interacting with the people and the resources around them and this has an unpredictable influence on their brains. We all know that the way pupils interact affects learning. We know that grouping pupils of different attainment levels gives different outcomes from grouping pupils with similar skill sets (Watson 1992; Thurston et al. 2010). We know that it is not just their understanding but the collaborative skills that children have that influence their success in group tasks (Baines et al. 2007). We know that the way they talk to each other is important (Mercer et al. 2004); that pupils can learn from watching each other (Bandura et al. 1966) and that different pupils bring different experiences and parental expectations. Bourdieu (1986) calls this 'cultural capital'. We also suspect that the weather influences children and if the lesson is before or after break. As Sampson and Clark (2009) concluded, the outcomes of pupil interaction depend upon the task and the context. To me, the joy of teaching is the unpredictable reactions, the strange conversations and the need to be responsive to what emerges. Yet educational theory does not seem to talk about this.

It is worth considering that what happens in the classroom is 'non-linear' and complex. The course of a lesson can change quickly and the 'character' or 'dynamic' of the class is sensitive to internal and external influences. Wegner et al. (1991) found that adult couples were able to remember a list of objects much better than people who had just met. They proposed that when people work or live together they take on a kind of 'social memory'. I was recently told by a teacher that her class was 'like a wolf pack' and they could work together to solve problems or devour an unsuspecting supply teacher.

How do teachers respond to classroom dynamics?

There is a growing, but still marginal, field of research looking at how we might describe classrooms as complex systems, drawing on a broad range of research in the sciences and social sciences. However, while the research catches up, I wish to put forward the case that teachers already know that learning is messy, sensitive and 'non-linear'. They might not be able to put it into words but experienced teachers have a 'feel' for their class and are constantly responding to the dynamics of that class. We might speculate that this is because teachers' brains also adapt to the class as they spend time with them. What I like about this way of looking at classrooms is that it values classroom experience in a way that very little educational theory does. It also tells us that classrooms are messy, complex and unpredictable, but the best thing that you can do as a teacher is to get involved.

References and further reading

Baines, E., Blatchford, P. and Chowne, A. (2007), 'Improving the effectiveness of collaborative group work in primary schools: Effects on science attainment', *British Educational Research Journal*, 33, (5), 663–80.

Bandura, A., Grusec, J. and Menlove, F. (1966), 'Observational Learning as a Function of Symbolization and Incentive Set', *Child Development*, 37, (3), 499–506.

Bourdieu, P. (1986), 'The Forms of Capital', in J. Richardson, (ed.), *Handbook for Theory and Research for the Sociology of Education*. Westport Connecticut: Greenwood Press, 241–58.

Brown, D. and Hammer, D. (2008), 'Conceptual change in physics', in S. Vosniadou (ed.), *International Handbook of Research on Conceptual Change*. New York: Routledge, 127–54.

Cilliers, P. (1998), *Complexity and Postmodernism: Understanding Complex Systems*. London: Routledge.

Department for Education (DfE) (2011), *The National Strategies 1997-2011 – A Brief Summary of the Impact and Effectiveness of the National Strategies*. London: DfE.

Freeman, W. (1999), *How Brains Make Up Their Minds*. London: Weidenfeld and Nicolson.

Kelso, J. (1995), *Dynamic Patterns: The Self-Organisation of Brain and Behaviour*. Cambridge, MA: MIT Press.

Mercer, N., Dawes, L., Wegerif, R. and Sams, C. (2004), 'Reasoning as a Scientist: Ways of Helping Children to Use Language to Learn Science', *British Educational Research Journal*, 30, (3), 359–77.

Richardson, J. (ed.) (1986), *Handbook for Theory and Research for the Sociology of Education*. New York: Greenwood Press.

Sampson, V. and Clark, D. (2009), 'The Impact of Collaboration on the Outcomes of Scientific Argumentation', *Science Education*, 93, (3), 448–84.

Thurston, J., Topping, K., Tolmie, A., Christie, D., Karagiannidou, E. and Murray, P. (2010), 'Cooperative learning in science: Follow-up from primary to secondary school', *International Journal of Science Education*, 32, (4), 501–22.

Watson, S. (1992), 'The Essential Elements of Cooperative Learning', *The American Biology Teacher*, 54, (2), 84–6.

Wegner, D., Raymond, P. and Erber, R. (1991), 'Transactive Memory in Close Relationships', *Journal of Personality and Social Psychology*, 61, (6), 923–9.

Vosniadou, S. (ed.) (2008), *International Handbook of Research on Conceptual Change*. Routledge: New York.

8 Do teachers deceive?

John-Paul Riordan

'It was only a joke!' said the culprit. This might be true from the perspective of this particular culprit, but is it possible that I could be deceived? I thought it looked like a fight, but it appears that I am mistaken and this was an amusing jest. The last sentence may be read with irony, or not. This chapter will explore how pupils and teachers deceive each other in school.

The etymology of the word 'deceive' (from the Latin *decipere*) suggests that something has been taken from us. So a fraudster, who takes my money by pretending to be from my bank, has deceived me. This is a crime, and not nice. Some deception in school is undoubtedly wrong. So a pupil who attempts to convince me that her dog has eaten her homework, with a straight face, is doing something wrong. But what if the same explanation is presented as a shared joke? Is that still deception? I will argue that deception is not always wrong in school, and that this is a tactic that we as teachers use fairly regularly.

Have you experienced something which might be described as 'deception' in school?

The Oxford English Dictionary defines deception as the attempt to persuade another that something false is actually true (Sykes 1988). This is to mislead someone deliberately, and according to this definition, to disappoint. This chapter adopts a different, and classic, definition of deception by Whaley (1982), who undertook a thorough investigation of war and magic. He saw deception as, 'a distortion of perceived reality' (p. 182). So, soldiers might perceive a wooden horse to be a friendly present from the enemy; David Blaine might persuade me that I am being entertained.

Do you ever deliberately distort the perception of another person? If so, how do you do this? What experiences, if any, do you have of your own perception being distorted?

Deception in school emerged as a theme during my PhD thesis (Riordan 2014) and the definition by Whaley quoted above proved useful in the interpretation of talk between small groups of pupils and their teachers. This chapter will draw on the data and findings of that study. Two kinds of deception are possible according to Whaley; dissimulation (hiding the real) and simulation (showing the false); both of which can be further subdivided. The three types of dissimulation are; masking (making invisible), repackaging (disguising) and dazzling (causing someone to lose clear vision). Three types of simulation are, mimicking (through imitation), inventing (displaying a different reality) and decoying (diverting attention).

Examples of these can be found commonly in school. Children often dissimulate by hiding, '1, 2, 3 . . . 7, 10, coming, ready or not' (masking). Dressing up is an important childhood experience (repackaging). Deliberately tormenting a teacher so that they lose their temper is used by some children to avoid working (dazzling). Many children love to pretend to be something they are not, like a smoking grown-up (mimicking); some like to strut across the playground as if they are models (displaying a fake reality). Few school criminals do not know that the attention of the teacher must be distracted while skulduggery is undertaken (diverting attention).

Teachers also appear to use all six types of deception (Riordan 2014: 146). For example, a common instructional technique is to hide an object in a 'mystery bag' (Spurlin 1995) so pupils must guess what it is (masking). My sister, an experienced science teacher, emerged from a cupboard in disguise as the pupils arrived in her classroom as 'Miss Riordan's evil twin sister' (repackaging). A teacher might 'turn on the charm' as a behaviour management technique (dazzling). Many teachers cannot resist taking part in class role-play (imitation). Teachers often pretend that compulsory classroom activities are 'games' (a different reality). Finally as disaster strikes, some colleagues might draw attention to something fascinating on the interactive whiteboard (decoy).

To what extent might Whaley's (1982) typology of deception be of use to you in interpreting your own experiences in school?

Teachers sometimes use deception to bring about learning. The following is an extract from Riordan (2014: 149) where an experienced science teacher (T) imitates a person who does not understand how to use a torch. CS, JB and BN are year 7 (11–12-year-old) pupils working in a group of six. They have been asked to imagine that they are in a completely dark room and describe how they see a teddy bear when they have a torch available:

T (teacher): . . . How do we get to see teddy?
CS: You see teddy by [shining? – unclear] the torch.
T: . . . I'm looking round [mimes looking left and right without moving the torch].

CS: . . . and you find it with the torch.

T: I'm looking around [as before].

T: I'm looking around. Can I see teddy?

BN: Use the torch! [Smiling]

CS: That's what I'm trying to say.

T: Oh, I'm moving the torch as well [as if surprised].

T: So I'm not just looking, I'm looking and moving the torch [mimes looking left while shining the torch to the right, then looking right while shining the torch to the left].

JB: [Laughs]

BN: Wait!

JB: You have the torch and your eyes [miming using his pen as the torch showing the torch being shone in the direction he is looking]. . . .

T: So I have to keep my eyes with . . . the light. Why? [Pulling a face as if T doesn't see the need for this.]

How do you interpret the above discussion?

In this passage the teacher pretends six times that she does not understand what to do. First she looks left and right, but doesn't move the torch, forcing the pupils to explain that both torch and eyes must move. Next she looks one way while shining the torch in the other direction, by which she indirectly points out to the pupils that their explanation is inadequate. Even when the teacher appears to understand what to do, she pretends that this requires an explanation. The laughs and smiles by pupils during this exchange indicate that at least some know what the teacher is doing. This experienced Advanced Skills Teacher poses as someone ignorant of how to use a torch (a well-known rhetorical technique called Socratic irony).

There is some literature exploring childhood deception (Salekin et al. 2008; Vasek 1985). Deception in the teaching profession has also been written about; Allen (2010) describes 'bluff activities'. Here, I would argue that the typology of deception developed by Whaley (1982) may be helpful for teachers in understanding their own practice, and the stratagems of the children in their care.

In what ways might investigating deception be problematic?

Interpretation of deception is inherently difficult, and misunderstanding is possible in many instances. Practitioners may have a natural hesitation to acknowledge what could be seen as deceptive activities (which in itself could be seen as dissimulation). But if experienced teachers are adept at not only managing the deception of pupils, but also deceive children in order to promote learning, this should be taken into account when exploring practice. Deception will always be hard to detect, but can become a powerful teaching tool, especially if it is done well.

References and further reading

Allen, M. (2010), 'Learner error, affectual stimulation, and conceptual change', *Journal of Research in Science Teaching*, 47, (2), 151–73.

Mitchell, R. and Thompson, N. (1986), *Deception: Perspectives on Human and Nonhuman Deceit (SUNY Series on Animal Behavior*. New York: State University of New York Press.

Riordan, J. (2014), *Techniques, Tactics and Strategies for Conceptual Change in School Science*, PhD Thesis, Canterbury Christ Church University (Unpublished).

Rogers, R. (2008), *Clinical Assessment of Malingering and Deception* (3rd edn). New York: Guilford Press.

Salekin, R., Kubak, F. and Lee, Z. (2008), 'Deception in children and adolescents', in R. Rogers (ed.), *Clinical Assessment of Malingering and Deception* (3rd edn). New York: Guilford Press, 343–64.

Spurlin, Q. (1995), 'Making science comprehensible for language minority students', *Journal of Science Teacher Education*, 6, (2), 71–8.

Sykes, J. (1988), *The Concise Oxford Dictionary of Current English* (7th edn). Oxford: Oxford University Press.

Vasek, M. (1985), 'Lying as a skill: The development of deception in children', in R. Mitchell and N. Thompson (eds), *Deception: Perspectives on Human and Nonhuman Deceit (SUNY Series on Animal Behavior)*. New York: State University of New York Press, 271–92.

Whaley, B. (1982), 'Toward a General Theory of Deception', *Journal of Strategic Studies*, 5, (1), 178–92.

9 Does assessment ensure learning?

Margaret Sangster

Test nursery children to help the poorest, says Ofsted chief.

(Daily Telegraph 21 June 2013: 8)

For some this headline will conjure up an alarming picture of 5-year-olds sitting in rows, silently completing exam papers. Hopefully this is not the case as the article goes on to say that Sir Michael Wilshaw is seeking 'assessment' of 5-year-olds and 'testing' of 7-year-olds. While it is an opportunity to consider the educational value of these approaches, the point to be made here is the importance of being clear about what is meant by assessment. When considering whether assessment ensures learning it is vital to clarify expectations of both 'assessment' and 'learning'.

Assessment could be defined as the gathering of information for the purpose of informing interested parties. Generally, this is termed 'summative' assessment.

When information is gathered in national tests (at seven and eleven in England), who are the interested parties?

Many (Black et al. 2003; Clarke 2001; Overall and Sangster 2006; Torrance and Pryor 1998) see assessment in broader terms than this. Information is gathered through several means such as observation, discussion with children, marking, testing, questioning and setting tasks. This information is then evaluated, either at the time or later, and subsequently action is taken by the teacher, or child, to improve understanding or to improve a skill. This has come to be known as formative assessment as it informs the learner of where they are and how they can progress in their learning.

Formative assessment gained credence in the 1990s through the work of Paul Black and his colleagues (Black and William 1998; Black et al. 2003). Many official organizations have adopted their approach (Primary National Strategy 2004; Ofsted 2008) and there is now considerable recent literature on practical approaches to formative assessment in the classroom (e.g. Looney

2010; NFER 2007). It does have its detractors. Dunn and Mulvenon (2009) carried out a critical review of research into formative assessment and concluded that scientifically most of the research methodology was not sound and, although there were probably positive outcomes to this way of working, nothing was proven. This might be considered somewhat harsh; as educational research is influenced by so many variables, it is impossible to eliminate them and providing a control group might be considered unethical or at the least detrimental to children's learning. A more positive 'observational view' is provided by Ofsted in their 2008 report.

As a teacher, in what ways have you used a cycle of gathering information, evaluating it and planning future learning?

If one recognizes that individuals have different rates of learning and different bodies of knowledge, then how is it possible to respond to 30 different needs in the classroom? Can you really provide 30 different mini lessons? This sounds like a recipe for the ideal, but impossible and probably not the best road to go down. But it does show that even with the most assiduous efforts it is difficult to ensure learning is taking place for all children all the time and the best that teachers can do is to maximize opportunities for individuals to learn.

Learning is a tricky thing in itself. If it is defined as a child experiencing something new then learning is occurring much of the time. If there is an expectation that the child will remember what he or she is experiencing then the elements of understanding and remembering become involved. Assessing learning as it takes place in the classroom could establish whether a child has understood a new experience. Assessing at a later date will establish whether the experience has entered long-term memory and can be produced in the right context. Testing and delayed assessments measure a child's ability to remember (recall) and even apply their learning in a new context. Some tests such as spelling and multiplication tables tests will demand direct regurgitation of facts, while other tests such as problem solving, comprehension and analysis require a much higher order of response. These latter tests require recognition of the situation (memory), possible realignment of the knowledge held (transfer) and application, usually through interpreting a language context. Richard Skemp, as far back as 1971, referred to these two types of learning as 'instrumental' and 'relational' learning; instrumental being similar to a learnt recipe, while relational indicated understanding of the context and an ability to apply knowledge. A child might have a piece of knowledge but fail to make the connection to a new situation. Does this mean the child has not learnt the original work?

Consider a topic you are planning to teach. What level of learning do you require and how will you assess that a child sufficiently understands the topic?

Some children will grasp new work quickly and comprehensively. Others will require several visits and may need several rehearsals before the work is established in long-term memory. This is where ongoing formative assessment has a role to play. Lessons need to be structured to allow all to engage and progress, including the able children. If everyone benefits from the objective, it is probably appropriate to have a whole class lesson; if children are at different stages, then probably group or individual work is appropriate for that lesson. Beyond that, the teacher differentiates through questioning and scaffolding strategies (Wood et al. 1976).

Some general strategies, which allow for formative assessment and which support learning, can be the way the teacher structures the interactions between the children and him- or herself – for example, marking using constructive comments and then allowing time when children get their work back so they can respond to mistakes and comments. This might be done as a whole class discussion or group or individual time. Children can be encouraged to participate in evaluating their own performance against success criteria (originally suggested by Shirley Clarke 2001). Often children are good at judging how they have performed and what they need. This is invaluable discourse. All teachers should have a repertoire of questioning types (Bloom 1956; Perrott 1982; Wragg and Brown 2001; Jeffcoat et al. 2004; Stone 2013) including higher order questions, which get children to think and construct links with existing knowledge. Rowe (1974) conducted a piece of research on response time, later utilized by Black et al. (2003), which showed that teachers rarely wait long enough for children to compose an answer before moving on. The Primary National Strategy (DfES 2004) advice of assessing formatively through observation, discussion with children, marking, testing, questioning and setting tasks, offers a balanced approach to assessing as part of the teaching cycle as opposed to assessment as a separate end-point activity.

Do you think you achieve a balance of teaching, assessment, evaluation and response in your classroom? What one thing would you choose to introduce today that would give you a better knowledge of the children's learning?

In response to the original question, it is my view that nothing 'ensures' learning; but assessment can 'enable' learning through an informed and purposeful use of a range of strategies.

References and further reading

Assessment Reform Group (2012), *Assessment for Learning: 10 principles*, http://assessmentreformgroup. files.wordpress.com/2012/01/10principles_english.pdf (accessed January 2014).

Black, P. and Wiliam, D. (1998), *Inside the Black Box: Raising Standards through Classroom Assessment*. London: School of Education, Kings College.

Black, P., Harrison, C., Lee, C., Marshall, B. and Wiliam, D. (2003), *Assessment for Learning: Putting it into Practice*. Maidenhead: Open University Press.

Bloom, B. (1956), *Taxonomy of Educational Objectives* (2 vols). New York: Longman Green.

Clarke, S. (2001), *Unlocking Formative Assessment*. London: Hodder and Stoughton.

DfES (2004), *Excellence and Enjoyment: Learning and Teaching in the Primary Years: Planning for Assessment for Learning*, Primary National Strategy DfES 0521-2004G. London: Crown copyright.

Dunn, K. and Mulvenon, S. (2009), 'A Critical View of Research on Formative Assessment: The Limited Scientific Evidence of the Impact of Formative Assessment in Education', *Practical Assessment, Research and Evaluation*, http://www.pareonline.net/pdf/v14n7.pdf (accessed January 2014).

Looney, J. (December 2010), 'Thinking Deeper in Assessment: Research Strategies Number 1 – part 3', *Making it Happen: Formative Assessment and Educational Technologies*, http://www. PrometheanWorld.com (accessed January 2014).

National Foundation for Educational Research (NFER) (2007), 'Starting out in Assessment', *Getting to Grips with Assessment: Primary* (series leaflet), http://www.nfer.ac.uk (accessed January 2014).

Jeffcoat, M., Jones, M., Mansergh, J., Mason, J., Sewell, H. and Watson, A. (2004), *Primary Questions and Prompts*. Derby: Association of Teachers of Mathematics (ATM).

Ofsted (2008), *Assessment for Learning: The Impact of National Strategy Support*, http://www.Ofsted.gov. uk (ref. 070244) (accessed January 2014).

Overall, L. and Sangster, M. (2006), *Assessment: A Practical Guide for Teachers*. London: Continuum.

Perrott, E. (1982), *A Practical Guide to Improving Your Teaching*. Harlow: Longman.

Primary National Strategy (2004), 'Part 4: Day to Day Assessment Strategies', *Excellence and Enjoyment: Learning and Teaching in the Primary Years: Planning and Assessment for Learning, Assessment for Learning* (DfES 0521-2004G), http://www.lancsngfl.ac.uk/curriculum/assessment/download/ file/04%20Day%20to%20Day%20Ass%20Strategies.pdf (accessed January 2014).

Rowe, M. (1974), 'Wait time and rewards as instructional variables, their influence on language, logic and fate control', *Journal of Research in Science Teaching*, 11, 81–94.

Sangster, M. (ed.) (2013), *Developing Teacher Expertise: Exploring Key Issues in Primary Practice*. London: Bloomsbury.

Skemp, R. (1971), *The Psychology of Learning Mathematics*. Harmondsworth: Penguin.

Stone, P. (2013), 'How can questioning create thoughtful reflection and learning in mathematics?', in M. Sangster (ed.), *Developing Teacher Expertise: Exploring Key Issues in Primary Practice*. London: Bloomsbury, 73–7.

Torrance H. and Pryor, J. (1998), *Investigating Formative Assessment*. Maidenhead: Open University Press.

Wilson, V. and Kendall-Seatter, S. (2010), *Developing Professional Practice 7-14*, Chapter 10. Harlow: Pearson Education, 212–33.

Wood, D., Bruner, J. and Ross, G. (1976), 'The role of tutoring in problem solving', *Journal of Child Psychology & Psychiatry & Allied Disciplines*, 17, (2), 89–100.

Wragg, E. and Brown, G. (2001), *Questioning in the Primary School*. London: Routledge.

Part II
Developing an Effective Curriculum

Each subject has its own curriculum/syllabus but there is an element of choice in how the subject is taught. This choice is influenced by resources, context, expectations and a teacher's own beliefs. This part questions how we teach subjects or even if we continue to teach them.

Are the arts good for children's health?

Jonathan Barnes

Inter-disciplinary research involving neuroscience, psychology, physiology and aspects of education aims to overcome barriers between education and health (Willington and Lloyd 2007; Howard Jones 2010, Hefferton 2013). Scientific research increasingly influences policy and practice towards children in the realms of advertising, product design, pharmaceuticals and policy making (Blakemore and Frith 2005; Greenfield 2010) but in Education such liaisons seem new. The arts have great potential to improve children's health but school arts are under threat in England.

Every 4 or 5 years the Trends in International Mathematics and Science Study (TIMSS) and the Programme for International Student Assessment (PISA) ratings compare easily measurable aspects of Maths, reading and science ability in young people across the developed world. Recent results showed England to be middle-ranking in its scores, and their publication (*The Guardian* 2013) initiated a frenzy of recriminations and demands for more focus on 'the basics'. More difficult-to-assess aspects of learning, for example in the arts, become side-lined as nations battle for supremacy in international rankings in the 'core subjects': English, mathematics and science (Alexander 2010b). Polarization of the education debate has resulted.

How do you see this reflected in your school?

'Traditional education' (Gove 2013) and 'creative education' (Driscoll et al. 2015) seem to oppose each other. The 'traditional' focuses on acquiring and frequently testing knowledge, memory and 'cultural capital' while creative learning is described by the now disbanded Qualifications and Curriculum Agency (QCA) as:

Questioning and challenging;
Making connections and seeing relationships;
Envisaging what might be;
Exploring ideas, keeping options open;
Reflecting critically on ideas, actions and outcomes. (QCA 2005)

What place do these five skills have in your teaching?

Traditional and creative methods easily combine however, and the arts offer examples of many successful fusions. Evidence shows the arts motivate and engage but can also generate deep learning, and personal well-being (Roberts 2006; PCAH 2011).

Personal well-being combines healthy self-esteem, emotional security, resilience, high degrees of satisfaction with friends, family, community, school and life in general (Csikszentmihalyi 2002; Seligman 2004; Huppert et al. 2005; Fredrickson 2009; NPC website). The improvement of well-being has become a focus of health and education policy especially since the publication of the Marmot Report (2010). This report revealed marked inequalities in health across British society especially for young people. International studies (WHO 2012; UNICEF 2013) also highlight poor mental and social health among UK youngsters. Education researchers have recognized child well-being as a crucial precondition of learning (Alexander 2010a and 2010b; Robinson and Aronica 2010).

The Arts have long been linked with personal and community well-being through their dependence on the personal, emotional, creative and on meaning-making. Aristotle for example argues,

> anger and mildness, courage and modesty, and their contraries, as well as all other dispositions of the mind, are most naturally imitated by music and poetry; which is plain by experience, for when we hear these our very soul is altered.
> (Aristotle, website)

The body responds to feelings of security, joy and satisfaction by functioning more efficiently. Perceptions of well-being impact on aspects of mental and social health: our capacity to learn, relate and feel resilient or content (Damasio 2003; Fredrickson 2009).

What specific strategies do you use to promote these qualities in your classroom?

The following four examples illustrate the health transformations arts can achieve.

Singing to confidence

Improved feelings of confidence and security were aims of the Haringey Lullabies Project (Barnes 2014b). In this year-long programme, a singer/songwriter worked with families and children attending nurseries in a deprived area of

London. The musician wrote and recorded bespoke lullabies for each of 80 children. Informal conversations with parents/carers, generated personalized lullaby lyrics, which included everything that mattered to the child: her toys, sayings, special words and people and a personal message from the carer. Each lullaby was taught to staff and children and their choruses sung almost daily in routine work around the nursery. CD recordings were given to parents/carers and played at home or in the car. Results from this project included measurable rises in self-assurance and security in some very vulnerable children; smoother, positive and more frequent liaison between nursery and parents/carers who reported positive behaviour change. Nursery practitioners recorded significantly improved speech, language and communication scores.

Continuing with communication

A drama intervention, the Speech Bubbles Project, was designed to support children with severe speech, language and communication difficulties. Throughout a year in inner city primary schools, drama practitioners worked with groups of ten referred children to make plays based upon verbatim stories related by each member. Chants summarizing the values of the group, warm-up activities and rehearsals preceded each performance. Results in 2012 showed that 89 per cent of children demonstrated improvements in learning, speaking and listening, 50 per cent were classed as having made 'clear' or 'striking' progress. Even greater changes were recorded in emotional behaviour and conduct, 65 per cent having made 'major and unexpected' improvements and a further 25 per cent having made 'some improvements' (London Bubble website). A follow-up study in 2013 found for a significant majority of children that gains in self-confidence, security, behaviour, motivation, relationships and speech, communication and language ability had transferred from a small group to everyday classroom settings (Barnes 2014a).

Dancing to health

Laban and Hampshire Dance combined to assess a 10-week creative dance programme in schools. Designed to address concerns about fitness and obesity in young people (Quin et al. 2007), the project emphasized creativity in movement because of its motivational and expressive possibilities. At the beginning and end of the programme, 11–14-year-olds were assessed on aspects of physiological and psychological health. Teaching on healthy hearts and bodies was incorporated within each session. Students expressed very positive responses to the course, but its physiological effects were the most striking. Statistically significant improvements in breathing, lung capacity, movement and aerobic fitness, occurred only in girls , (boys showed only small physical improvements). Girls showed an average 44 per cent improvement in aerobic fitness, suggesting a major positive health impact on a population typically reluctant to join in sports activities. Both genders showed improvements in psychological health but the greatest change was in their attitudes towards dancing; 67 per cent claimed to view dancing positively and were motivated towards dance. Well-being measures showed that dance promoted improvements in self-esteem and general motivation towards school in all children.

Art and coping with pain

Research linking art (such as painting, drawing, collage and digital image making) with well-being usually comes from art therapy. Art has been used in many cultures, to help individuals visualize, control feelings, fears, pains and develop calming mechanisms. Art therapy similarly helps children express thoughts, feelings and memories difficult or impossible to express in words. Studies show that children facing frequent painful medical procedures specifically benefit from involvement in art making. For example, research of 2–14-year-olds found how children with leukaemia showed significantly enhanced capacities to cope during and after lumbar punctures when given the opportunity to draw or do other art activities before, during and after the painful procedure (Favara-Scacco et al. 2001). The randomized control study showed significantly increased coping mechanisms, collaboration, enhanced capacity to adapt and accept hospitalization and fewer signs of trauma among those involved in art-making. The paediatricians' explanation for these remarkable effects has implications for art in all settings with children.

> Art Therapy modalities intensify activity in the brain's right side, stimulating imagination and creative symbolisation and facilitating the brain's capacity to concentrate on pleasurable thoughts. This stimulation enables the young patient to relax, and to reduce the level of anxiety. (Favara-Scocco 2001: 475)

These case studies exemplify the special qualities of the arts to involve children at an emotional level, provide opportunities for nonverbal communication and enhance quality of life for young people. They used arts practitioners, with high subject expectations, passionate about preserving the unique qualities of their discipline. Combining the expressive, creative qualities of their art with high expectations and good subject knowledge, each practitioner generated measurable well-being among children. But research into the arts and well-being in schools is rare. Classroom research, especially randomized control studies, will provide evidence that will help the arts gain their rightful position as the humanizing and health-giving subjects.

References and further reading

Alexander, R. (2010a), *Children, Their World, Their Education.* Cambridge: Cambridge University Press.

—(2010b), '"World class schools" – noble aspiration or globalised hokum?' *Compare: A Journal of Comparative and International Education,* 40, (6), 801–17, DOI: 10.1080/03057925.2010.523252.

Aristotle, *Politics,* Book VIII Chapter 5, http://aristotle.thefreelibrary.com/A-Treatise-on-Government/7-5 (accessed March 2014).

Barnes, J. (2014a), 'Drama to promote well-being in 6 and 7 year olds with language and communication difficulties: The Speech Bubbles Project', *Perspectives in Public Health,* 134, (2), 103–12.

—(2014b), *The Haringey Lullabies Project: Music Enhancing Health and Education Outcomes in an Early Years Setting.* Report published by the Sidney de Haan Research Centre for Arts and Health, Folkestone.

Blakemore, S-J. and Frith, U. (2005), *The Learning Brain.* London: Wiley-Blackmore.

Csikszentmihalyi, M. (2002), *Flow: The Classic Work on how to Achieve Happiness.* New York: Ebury Press.

Damasio, A. (2003), *Looking for Spinoza: Joy Sorrow and the Feeling Brain.* New York: Harcourt.

Driscoll, P., Lambirth, A. and Roden, J. (2015), *The Creative Primary Curriculum.* London: Routledge.

Favara-Scacco, C., Smirne, G. and Di Cataldo, A. (2001), 'Art therapy and painful procedures in Leukaemia', *Paediatric Blood and Cancer,* 36, (4), 474–80.

Fredrickson, B. (2009), *Positivity.* New York: Crown.

Geake, J. (2009), *The Brain at School.* Maidenhead: Open University Press.

Gove, M. (2013), *Why Traditional Education is a Work of Social Justice – One that I am Striving to Deliver,* http://www.conservativehome.com/platform/2013/09/michael-gove-mp-2.html (accessed February 2014).

Greenfield, S. (2003), *Tomorrows Children.* London: Penguin.

—(2010), *You and Me.* London: Notting Hill.

Guardian, (The) (2013), Tuesday 3 December 2013, http://www.theguardian.com/education/2013/dec/03/uk-students-education-oecd-pisa-report (accessed March 2014).

Hefferton, K. (2013), *Positive Psychology and the Body: The Somatopsychic Side of Flourishing.* Maidenhead: Open University Press.

Howard-Jones, P. (2010), *Introducing Neuroeducational Research: Neuroscience, Education and the Brain.* London: Routledge.

Huppert, F., Keverne, B. and Baylis, N. (2005), *The Science of Well-Being*. Oxford: Oxford University Press.

London Bubble website (2013), *Speech Bubbles Report 2013*, http://www.londonbubble.org.uk/uploads/Year%204%20report%20-%20FINAL.pdf (accessed March 2014).

Marmot, M. (Sir) (2010), Report to UK Government, *Fair Society: Healthy Lives*,http://www.instituteofhealthequity.org/projects/fair-society-healthy-lives-the-marmot-review (accessed October 2013).

New Philanthropy Capital (NPC), http://www.thinknpc.org/ (accessed March 2014).

PCAH (President's Committee on Arts and Humanities) (2011), *Reinvesting in Arts Education: Winning America's Future through Creative Schools*, http://www.pcah.gov/resources/re-investing-arts-educationwinning-americas-future-through-creative-schools (accessed March 2014).

Programme for International Student Assessment (PISA) website (2013), http://www.oecd-ilibrary.org/sites/factbook-2013-en/10/01/01/index.html?itemId=/content/chapter/factbook-2013-72-en (accessed March 2014).

Qualifications and Curriculum Authority (QCA), http://www.teachfind.com/qcda/creativity-find-it-promote-it (accessed March 2014).

Quin, E., Frazer, L. and Redding, E. (2007), 'The health benefits of creative dance: Improving children's physical and psychological well-being', *Education and Health*, 25, (2), 31–3.

Roberts, P. (2006), *Nurturing Creativity in Young People: A Report to Government to Inform Future Policy*. London: Department for Culture, Media and Sport.

Robinson, K. and Aronica, L. (2010), *The Element: How Finding Your Passion Changes Everything*, London: Penguin.

Seligman, M. (2004), *Authentic Happiness*. New York: Basic Books.

Trends in International Mathematics and Science Study (TIMSS), http://timssandpirls.bc.edu/ (accessed March 2014).

United Nations International Children's Emergency Fund (UNICEF) (2013), *Innocenti Report Card*, http://www.unicef.org.uk/Latest/Publications/Report-Card-11-Child-well-being-in-rich-countries/ (accessed March 2014).

Willington, D. and Lloyd, J. (2007), 'How educational theories can use neuroscientific data', *Mind Brain and Education*, 1, (3), 140–9.

World Health Organization (WHO) (2012), *Social Determinates of Health and Well-being among Young People*, http://www.euro.who.int/__data/assets/pdf_file/0003/163857/Social-determinants-of-health-and-well-being-among-young-people.pdf (accessed March 2014).

Is there a 'place' for geography in the curriculum? 11

Terry Whyte

Geography is categorized as a 'foundation' subject in the 2014 National Curriculum in England (DfE 2013). This is an indication, perhaps, of the importance of the subject; surely you build upon foundations. Don't you? Having a good geographical knowledge by the time children leave the primary stage allows them to . . . , well, to do what exactly?

What does studying geography add to a child's learning in these formative years?

What does Geography mean to you?

With all subject areas, we have experiences that shape our opinion of what to expect when learning and indeed teaching in that area of the curriculum. Many students associate Geography with their past experience of being taught the subject at secondary school and for some how to answer that tricky geographical quiz question on a television game show! Often past school experiences are related to shading in maps, drawing in blue around the coast and knowing where places are. It might also have been associated with unconnected, unimaginative, didactic teaching as reported by Ofsted Inspectors in 2011 when they reported that, 'Uninspiring teaching and the lack of challenge discouraged many students from choosing geography at GCSE' (p. 6).

If the past experience of many prospective primary school teachers is negative, it is not unreasonable for them to teach in a similar way to the way they were taught or to avoid the subject completely by citing a lack of confidence and knowledge. It is common for students on their first foray into the subject in training to fear engagement in geography. Thankfully, many are surprised to see what primary geography can be and begin to see the subject in a different light. Perhaps there is a need to define or redefine in our minds exactly what the subject stands for in order to justify its place as one of the foundation subjects in the curriculum.

Can you define Geography?

If you break up the words '*geo*' and '*graphia*' you are left with Greek derivations meaning 'Earth' and 'writing' . . . or perhaps 'earth description'? Geography then could be said to be about 'describing and interpreting our surroundings both local and distant' (Scoffham 2010: 9). If we take this definition on board, geography allows us and the children to explore the world around us, and beyond, and maybe could be said to be the most important subject in the world.

Is it just about knowing where places are or shading areas on a map?

Michael Palin (2007: 22), the comedian, actor and television explorer sees geography as more than this, 'a living, breathing subject, constantly adapting itself to change. It is dynamic and relevant. For me geography is a great adventure with a purpose'. But is it just about exploring? Well it could be but not necessarily on the scale that Michael Palin has been lucky enough to experience. Exploring can include not only observing unknown habitats, frozen wastes, lost peoples, ocean routes but also exploring our own environment. This is something we, Michael and children can actively do.

Being aware of the world around us is part of geographical thinking. Instead of needing to look for a specific geographical perspective, geography can be part of our everyday lives. 'Everyday geography' (Martin 2006) can be our 'routine geography', which Moran (2008) suggests is very much 'invisible'. Children's everyday lives are influenced by geography. We live on a planet spinning in space around a sun which gives us days and nights, seasons and weather. Waking up every morning is an element of being part of geography as children at home are living in their particular space, in a place, in a part of that world. Their breakfast would have been created by other people and sourced from local and faraway places in the world. Watching morning television brings that world into their homes from satellites far above the Earth.

The journey to school will always be different each day and follow routes which cross with those of other people and might use a form of transport across a variety of terrains. Playing in the playground might involve meeting children with a mix of ethnic origins and languages; it could involve using directions and territories. The clothes children wear originate from distant places and the stories children relate to each other reflect not just their place in the world but also their understanding of local and distant places.

Reading a book in class can trigger imagination of all sorts of locations with all sorts of characters, local and global. The children in all classrooms are connected with other children worldwide whether directly through families, internet chats with partnership schools or indirectly by associating themselves with the likes, dislikes, similarities and differences of children in other parts of the world. Learning in all subject areas allows a building of skills and knowledge that will equip these children with life in *their* world.

Geography has been defined as the interaction between people and places; how many times in one day do we refer to people and places?

It is when we, and children, begin to think in this way, that geography becomes a meaningful and relevant 'subject' in any curriculum; indeed it, 'is novel, fascinating, wondrous and important' (Catling and Willy 2009: 9). Scoffham (2010: 9) believes geography 'is as valid today as it was over 2000 years ago'.

In studying good Primary Geography, children can practise their reading skills and improve their spatial understanding through drawing and interpreting maps. Fieldwork enables children to explore their surroundings and recording and processing data gives purpose to their information technology skills (ICT). Enquiry is a key geographical skill and helps children to ask questions about what they see around them and beyond. All of these skills and a good knowledge of place, both local and global, can assist children in gaining 'a deeper understanding of processes that underpin both physical events and human activity' (Scoffham 2013: 9).

Geography shapes our world, is all around us and children are interconnected with this world; surely it is a true 'foundation subject'. The aims of the new Curriculum in England (DfE 2013: 1) mentions, 'A high-quality geography education should inspire in pupils a curiosity and fascination about the world and its people that will remain with them for the rest of their lives'. This is a noble aim, ensuring Geography, which is about places, has its *place* in the Curriculum!

References and further reading

Catling, S. and Willy, T. (2009), *Teaching Primary Geography*. Exeter: Learning Matters.

Department for Education (DfE) (2013), *National Curriculum in England: Primary curriculum*. London: HMSO.

Martin, F. (2006), *Teaching Geography in Primary Schools: Learning how to Live in the World*. Cambridge: Chris Kington.

Moran, J. (2008), *Queuing for Beginners: The Story of Daily Life from Breakfast to Bedtime*. London: Profile Books.

Ofsted (2011), *Geography-Learning to make a World of Difference*. London: HMSO.

Palin, M. (2007), 'Celebrating the Action Plan for Geography', *GA, Magazine of the Geographical Association*, 8, Spring 2008, Sheffield: Geographical Association, p. 22.

Scoffham, S. (ed.) (2010), *Primary Geography Handbook*. Sheffield: Geographical Association.

—(2013), *Teaching Geography Creatively*. London: Routledge.

Can break times help children's physical activity levels? 12
Kristy Howells

Break times and lunch times (collectively referred to here as break times) within a primary school are unstructured opportunities for children to engage in physical activity opportunities according to Johns and Ha (1999). Sarkin et al. (1997) suggested that girls and boys have the same opportunities to be physically active, this equality occurs especially within a primary school setting. Fairclough and Stratton (2005) observed boys reaching higher physical activity levels than girls. Trost et al. (2002) proposed similar results and found that boys were involved in significantly more moderate-to-vigorous physical activity than girls, during break times. These results may be linked to gender social constructions and male dominance in the playground. Connolly (2003) also suggested that a difference in break time activities could be due to gender segregation during break time, with the social construction of gender being evident in the active play of children during break time. He also proposed that there is a male dominance in the playground (Connolly 2003). Yet, Mota et al. (2005) found the opposite result with girls completing more moderate to vigorous physical activity (MVPA) than boys, although they did highlight the importance of break times as opportunities for all children to be physically active.

Do these findings agree with your observations of children's movement during break times?

Ridgers et al. (2006) stated that 'playtime can contribute between 5 and 40% of the recommended daily physical activity levels when no interventions have been utilised' (p. 359). While Pate et al. (1996) suggested that 'children best accumulate physical activity during playtime and in unstructured environments, where they are free to interact with their peers' (p. 96), Wellard (2012) identified outside environments as settings for children to enjoy moving and using their bodies, beyond just being physically active. Stratton and Leonard (2002) suggested that the playground is a key context in which children could engage physically on a daily basis for the majority of the whole school year other than wet play days, in which the children remain indoors within the primary school setting.

From your knowledge of children, have you noticed other benefits to children having break times?

Dau (1999) proposed that break times were also important for developing children socially and emotionally as well as physically. Pellegrini and Davis (1993) also identified other important aspects of break times: indicating that a lack of break time had a negative impact on children's performance in the classroom, with children becoming less attentive to both the tasks at hand and learning in general. Grugeon (2005) suggested that children's play during break time was important in developing children's literacy skills, such as the communication skills of listening and speaking. There are also opportunities to develop emotionally (Blatchford and Baines 2006) and socially in a positive way (Adams 1993) during break time. Blatchford and Sumpner, (1998) emphasized the value of break times as time to 'let off steam' (p. 92). Ridgers et al. (2011) suggested that the 'majority of children's social interactions were positive' within the primary school setting during break time, and that the removal of break times could 'influence both physical and social health' detrimentally (p. 364). Ramstetter et al. (2010) emphasized the idea that break times could promote activity and a 'healthy lifestyle' (p. 524) and highlighted the importance of break times in contributing to a child's creative, social and emotional development as well as their physical development.

How could you encourage children to be more active during break times?

One way to increase the levels of children's physical activity within the school day is by developing playground play by improving the play time environment, in order to help tackle inactivity, boredom and poor behaviour (Brady et al. 2008). This is particularly important as children, especially infants have been shown to, spend up to a quarter of their school day in the playground (Ridgers et al. 2006). Kent County Council (KCC) (2006), for example, suggested that physical activity could be improved through their playground improvement scheme. KCC (2006: 1) gave schools grants of £5,000 each to add facilities to school playgrounds that would 'increase sporting opportunities, develop skills-based activities and raise levels of physical activity.' KCCs (2006) evaluation found that 83 per cent of schools within the scheme stated that through the grant, they had increased sporting opportunities during playtime and that this had led to greater physical activity. Movement and physical activity around the playground could be encouraged through the use of simple additions of brightly coloured markings on the playground and interesting and exciting new additions such as playground and adventure equipment. These additions encouraged children to participate in 'running, jumping and balance' ultimately helping to 'develop stamina, suppleness and flexibility' (KCC 2006: 1). Stratton (2000) found that physical activity levels increased when fluorescent markings where used on school playgrounds.

Which resources do girls access and which resources do boys use?

It is doubtful that physical activity can be achieved during playtime in the future, especially if schools are built in a similar manner to those, for example, in East of England, which are built without playgrounds, or play areas and neglect the importance of play as a consideration (Beckford 2007). The charity, Fields in Trust (2011), reported that outdoor recreational spaces such as playing fields on school sites were under threat particularly during difficult economic times, and planning applications to build on such playing fields had more than doubled since 1999 when there were 625 applications to 1,322 applications in 2009. At the aforementioned rate, there would soon be neither playing fields nor playgrounds in schools as they would only have to provide suitable outdoor space, rather than as the previous strict rules stated, space that was dependent on the number of children at the school and of an area of at least 5,000 square metres (Harrison 2012).

Does your school have adequate, good or poor playing facilities and how could you improve them?

In conclusion, break times can contribute to physical activity levels of children within a primary school setting, and in particular allow moderate-to-vigorous levels of physical activity which will aid health benefits and link to the recommended daily physical activity levels of the child (WHO 2010). However, caution is needed in terms of the planning and building of new schools and allowing space for playgrounds to enhance not only the physical benefits but also the social, emotional and moral well-being of the children.

The aim of this chapter was to highlight what could be happening within break times within your primary school setting. Therefore, some areas to consider within your own professional practice, to observe what is happening at break time and to answer are as follows:

What is happening at break times in terms of physical activity levels?

Do you think that you would be able to identify the different intensity levels of physical activity? If so how can you tell the differences?

What differences are there between boys and girls, in terms of physical activity? How and what equipment are they accessing?

What is the most challenging activity available during break times for children and how many access it?

References and further reading

Adams, E. (1993), 'Schools out! New initiative for British school rounds', *Children's Environments*, 10, (2), 118–35

Adams, P. (2007), 'Learning and caring in the age of the five outcomes', *Education 3-13*, 35, (3), 225–37.

Beckford, M. (2007), *School Without Play Area Bans Break Times*, http://www.telegraph.co.uk/news/uknews/1550808/School-without-play-area-bans-break-times.html (accessed December 2007).

Blatchford, P. and Baines, E. (2006), *A Follow Up National Survey of Breaktimes in Primary and Secondary Schools. Report to The Nuffield Foundation*. London: Institute of Education.

Blatchford, P. and Sumpner, C. (1998), 'What do we know about breaktime? Results from a national survey of breaktime and lunchtime in primary and secondary schools', *British Educational Research Journal*, 24, (1), 79–94.

Brady, L., Gibb, J., Henshall, A. and Lewis, J. (2008), *Play and Exercise in Early Years: Physically Active Play in Early Childhood Provision*. London: Department for Culture, Media and Sport.

Connolly, P. (2003), 'Gendered and gendering spaces: Playgrounds in the early years', in C. Skelton and B. Francis (eds), *Boys and Girls in the Primary Classroom*. Maidenhead: Open University Press, Chapter 7, 113–33.

Dau, E. (1999), *Child's Play: Revisiting Play in Early Childhood Settings*. Sydney: Maclennan and Petty.

Fairclough, S. and Stratton, G. (2005), 'Physical education makes you fit and healthy: Physical education's contribution to young people's physical activity levels', *Health Education Research*, 20 (1), 14–23.

Fields in Trust (2011), *Loss of Sites*, http://www.fieldsintrust.org/Loss_of_Sites.aspx (accessed January 2012).

Grugeon, E. (2005), 'Listening to learning outside the classroom: Student teachers study playground literacies', *Literacy*, 39, (1), 3–9.

Harrison, A. (2012), *School Playing Fields: 31 Sales Approved*, http://www.bbc.co.uk/news/uk-19291911 (accessed December 2012).

Johns, D. and Ha, A. (1999), 'Home and recess physical activity of Hong Kong children', *Research Quarterly for Exercise and Sport*, 70, (3), 319–23.

Kent County Council (KCC) (2006), *PE and School Sport, Playground Improvement Scheme, Impact and Monitoring Report*," http://209.85.229.132/search?q=cache:XZZ70sYYdygJ:www.kentsport.org/schools/documents/PlaygroundMonitoringReportex-photos.doc+kent+children%27s+physical+activity+levels&cd=3&hl=en&ct=clnk&gl=uk, Kent County Council, Sports Development Unit (accessed October 2009).

Mota, J., Silva, P., Santos, M., Ribeiro, J., Oliveira, J. and Durate, J. (2005), 'Physical activity and school recess time: Difference between the sexes and the relationship between children's playground physical activity and habitual physical activity', *Journal of Sports Science*, 23, (3), 269–75.

Pate, R., Baranowski, T., Dowda, M. and Trost, S. (1996), 'Tracking of physical activity in young children', *Medicine Science Sport Exercise*, 28, (1), 92–6.

Pellegrini, A. and Davis, P. (1993), 'Relations between children's playground and recess behaviour', *British Journal of Educational Psychology*, 63, (1), 88–95.

Ramstetter, C., Murray, R. and Garner, A. (2010), 'The crucial role of recess in schools', *The Journal of School Health*, 80, (11), 517–26.

Ridgers, N., Carter, L., Stratton, G. and McKenzie, T. (2011), 'Examining children's physical activity and play behaviours during playtime over time', *Health Education Research*, 26, (4), 586–95.

Ridgers, N., Stratton, G. and Fairclough, S. (2006), 'Physical activity levels of children during school playtime', *Sports Medicine*, 36, (4), 359–71.

Sarkin, J., McKenzie, T. and Sallis, J. (1997), 'Gender differences in physical activity during fifth-grade physical education and recess period', *Journal of Teaching Physical Education*, 17, (1), 99–106.

Skelton, C. and Francis, B. (eds) (2003), *Boys and Girls in the Primary Classroom*. Maidenhead: Open University Press.

Stratton, G. (2000), 'Promoting children's physical activity in primary school: An intervention study using playground markings', *Ergonomics*, 43, (10), 1538–46.

Stratton, G. and Leonard, J. (2002), 'The effects of playground markings on the energy expenditure of 5 – 7 year old school children', *Paediatric Exercise Science*, 14, 170–80.

Trost, S., Pate, R., Sallis, J., Freedson, P., Taylor, W., Dowda, M. and Sirad, J. (2002), 'Age and gender differences in objectively measured physical activity in youth', *Medicine and Science in Sports and Exercise*, 34, 350–5.

Wellard, I. (2012), 'Body-reflexive pleasures: Exploring bodily experiences within the context of sport and physical activity', *Sport, Education and Society*, 17, (1), 21–33.

World Health Organisation (WHO) (2010), *Global Recommendations on Physical Activity For Health*, http://whqlibdoc.who.int/publications/2010/9789241599979_eng.pdf (accessed October 2010).

13

Why should primary mathematics teaching be set within the context of children's shared life experiences?

Jill Matthews

The beauty of mathematics lies in the patterns it explains; its usefulness lies in providing a precise language with which to explain our world and how it provides us with a tool to resolve everyday problems using various routes to derive the same answer. We only need the confidence to apply our knowledge in practice. And therein lies the problem; confidence or rather the apparent lack of confidence shared by a large proportion of the population renders them unwilling to attempt seemingly basic mathematical problems which are part of their everyday lives.

My argument rests on the fact that children need to acquire mathematical language in the same way as they acquire mastery of language, another symbolic system of communication. I believe that the ability to use and understand the language of mathematics is achieved through social interaction within the context of the life experiences children share with others. Ryan and Williams (2007) suggest that mathematics teaching and learning should 'be embedded within everyday knowledge and activity' (p. 153). We should help children to develop, not only conceptual understanding but also secure cognitive connections. They need to be able to apply that understanding to different situations and make links between the learning of mathematics in their homes with the learning at school. They need to be able to manipulate and articulate their mathematical understanding so that they can apply it to various situations.

To what extent does discussion form part of your children's mathematical learning?

It is vital, therefore, that, through their mathematical experiences within the 's group, children establish a common framework of shared understanding. is way they can socially construct their mathematical knowledge. Children 1 any primary school come from a range of socio-economic backgrounds and have an infinite variety of life experiences. Roulston et al. (2010) found that some 7 per cent of children start school with a language delay and are unable to construct proper sentences in their spoken language. This proportion is significantly higher in areas of social and economic deprivation. Time needs to be given to create a positive social and emotional climate, which will enable all children to develop positive behaviours and positive attitudes which will lead to effective collaborative learning. Failure to create such a positive ethos can create barriers to some children's learning.

How much time do you give to creating a collaborative working ethos within your classroom and does it extend to mathematics lessons?

Time needs to be given for all children within a class to become familiar with mathematical language and to develop the facility to understand it and to use it appropriately within the context of learning mathematics. Mathematical vocabulary needs to be used precisely, consistently and frequently. Cockcroft (1982) emphasized that the primary mathematics curriculum should 'enrich children's aesthetic and linguistic experience' (para. 287), and that 'practical work is essential throughout the primary years' (para. 289). Children should have time to manipulate the patterns of number, using resources, both physical and visual, to support their thinking as appropriate. Learning should be interactive between the teacher and pupil(s) or, between pupil and pupil. Children should be encouraged to articulate their understanding and to discuss each other's reasoning.

More attention should be given to the critical 'relationship of *interactive pace* to (the pace of) cognition and learning' (Alexander et al. 2010) and to providing extended opportunities for pupils to express their thinking. With this approach, the teacher's role becomes one of facilitating that extended dialogue rather than didactic transmission. Difficulties arise when 'pace' becomes more important than group cohesion. The current policy and the drive to improve standards seem to suggest that 'extending the higher achievers' carries more weight that ensuring that all pupils are able to achieve a secure understanding and progress together. This can create a situation where the teaching and activities are above the heads of many of the group with the consequence that some children struggle to understand, become disaffected and give up.

Wiliam (1999) suggests that formative assessment has the power to change the 'distribution of attainment', disproportionately benefiting the lower attainers. This is because the teacher is able to pitch the lesson to maximize children's access to the intended learning outcome. When children are encouraged and have the confidence to present their preferred method for calculating a particular answer and then to respond to questions from their peers, who may have used alternative methods, there is the possibility of rich discussion about the mathematics. Verbalization clarifies thinking and facilitates extended learning. Deeper understanding of why various methods provide the same solution extends children's mathematical thinking and encourages them to try alternative strategies. Teaching an algorithm without the child understanding why it works can hinder their mathematical progress.

Consider these examples:

> A final year teacher education student was teaching 5-year-olds about three-dimensional shapes. It was a whizzy lesson and the student was expertly using a PowerPoint presentation as a visual stimulus. The children were generally focussed on the screen and paying attention. Lots of questions were posed and some children responded using the correct vocabulary. The interaction was led by the teacher with the usual teacher-initiated questions, pupil responses followed by teacher affirmation (Sinclair and Coulthard 1975). The follow-up activity was a cut, stick and label exercise in workbooks. The children did not have the opportunity to handle a variety of objects, compare them or discuss what they had noticed.

Do you think they learned what was expected? Do you think it was appropriate to use computer images for this topic?

> A mature student said she had initially failed her GCSE (exam for the 16-year-olds) mathematics paper. In her secondary school (11–16 years), pupils were expected to work on their own using textbook exercises. Although she had enjoyed mathematics at primary school (5–11 years), since she went to secondary school she had always had difficulty with mathematics if she could not visualize what was happening. Without that visual conceptual understanding she could not remember a practised algorithm beyond the lesson when she had used it.

When do you think children should be introduced and asked to use an algorithm? When should they be asked to learn independently?

> When I asked a group of Malaysian ITE students to find 17.5% of £25 all 30 students did a formal long multiplication, most achieving the correct answer. No one divided 17.5 by 4. No one found the sum of 10%, then 5% and 2.5% of £25. So how did the students react when we discussed the alternative methods? There were some 'Aha!' moments when they looked at the numbers more closely. One student said that he had been taught how to do the algorithm, so that was how he approached it; it was the correct procedure.

What are the advantages and disadvantages of informal alternative methods which are used in real-life situations?

I believe children should have the opportunity to participate actively in their learning of mathematics. Working collaboratively in friendship groups to solve puzzles, problems with definite solutions and practical application in real-life situations makes the learning of mathematics purposeful, meaningful and enjoyable. The teacher's role should be to build on children's prior knowledge, facilitate discussion about the mathematics they use and to extend children's thinking. I believe they should try to maximize class cohesion and ensure all primary children have a secure understanding of number and basic arithmetic. Time needs to be given to create a positive learning ethos which can be enjoyed by all children and enable them to contribute constructively and with confidence.

References and further reading

Alexander, R. (2010), *Children, Their World, Their Education*. Abingdon: Routledge.

Cockcroft, W. (1982), *Mathematics Counts*. London: HMSO.

Roulston, S., Law, J., Rush, R., Clegg, J. and Peters, T. (2010), *Investigating the Role of Language in Children's Early Educational Outcomes*. Research Report DFE- RR134. London: DfE, https://www.gov.uk/government/publications/investigating-the-role-of-language-in-childrens-early-educational-outcomes (accessed March 2014).

Ryan, J. and Williams, J. (2007), *Children's Mathematics 4 - 15*. Maidenhead: Open University Press.

Sinclair, J. and Coulthard, R. (1975), *English Language: Interaction Analysis in Education; Study and Teaching*. London: Oxford University Press.

Wiliam, D. (Spring 1999), *Equals: Mathematics and Special Educational Needs*, 5, (2), 15–18, http://eprints.ioe.ac.uk/1150/1/Wiliam1999Formativepart115.pdf (accessed March 2014).

Why is it so difficult to learn a second language in English schools?

14

Victoria Schulze

◄───►

'Language learning is hard work'   *'Language learning is easy'*

If the degree of perceived difficulty of learning a new language is set along such a continuum, there could be many things that affect where we may place ourselves on it. The environment in which we learn a new language is likely to be one such factor. It is therefore important to reflect upon exactly how conducive to foreign language learning our school environments are, in order that we can better support primary pupils in making 'substantial progress' (DfE 2013; Tinsley 2013). Watkins (1999: 5) suggested that the classroom environment is 'the most complex and least understood situation on the face of the planet', warranting further investigation in relation to language learning. Indeed, Sharpe (2001) argues that primary schools are much better placed by virtue of their form and organization to deliver a programme of communicative competence than the secondary schools which have been actually charged with it. He claims, 'Teaching within an integrationist environment transforms the significance for pupils of what is learnt and can potentially raise standards of achievement and motivation' (p. 17). However, it remains questionable exactly how well these aims have been since realized, and how much instead has been invested in generating and relying upon an 'elite corps of primary modern foreign language (MFL) specialists' (Sharpe 1999: 132). The role that the physical structure of the classroom can play in influencing and motivating language learning has also been posed by the European Quality Education and Language Competencies for twenty-first-century Society: 'Traditions, Challenges, Visions' Conference (ECML 2014); the time is ripe to consider exactly what makes a good foreign language learning environment in our primary schools.

That young language learners 'just get on with language learning' in a largely unproblematic way that most adults do not, is argued by Wray (2008: 266–7).

Opportunities for pupils to simply 'get on with language learning' in their everyday experiences in school would therefore appear necessary. Meighan (in Gilbert 2013: 123) cautions that 'it is the way children are subjected to artificial made-up subjects that are not embedded in cultural practice which renders most school learning tedious and irrelevant'. Environments which only afford pupils opportunity to learn and use a language within a discrete foreign language lesson remain insufficient. Whether a foreign language can even be regarded as a 'subject' is questioned by Gilbert (2013: 124) who argues, 'French, why, that's not even a subject at all! It's a medium, a means to an end'. Viewed in this way, it should not be assumed that learning environments designed to support the learning of 'subjects' are equally as effective as those required to support the learning of a 'medium'.

If languages are viewed as a 'medium' rather than a 'subject', in which ways could the learning environment be adapted?

Learning a language directly in a country where it is spoken is often regarded as the best and certainly fastest way for most learners (Frigols et al. 2008). Learners can be naturally immersed in both language and culture, surrounded by the sights, sounds, scents, tastes and feel of their location. Learning a language in such a natural environment can not only be a truly holistic sensory experience, but such learning is also underpinned by potentially strong extrinsic and intrinsic motivational forces for the learner to actively understand, and be understood (Csizér and Dörnyei 2005). Such learning can indeed appeal to the learner's 'context', rather than 'content memory' as identified by Gilbert (2013: 127), thereby improving learning; 'real life leads to real learning' (Gilbert, ibid.).

Reflecting upon the continuum presented at the beginning, do you agree learning languages in such a natural environment could be 'easier' and more effective?

The primary school environment in England is generally a bright, colourful and vibrant one – full of varied displays, resources, artefacts, signs and posters; schools are busy places with the hustle and bustle of learning and everyday routine. However, in contrast to such richness, is the diet of school language learning assailing children's senses within these environments? Primary schools in England also embody tightly managed and structured environments, with pressures for pupils to excel in the core subjects. Time for the learning and teaching of languages can have clear limitations (Cable et al. 2010); even the range of language learnt can, at best, be sometimes described as 'just in case' rather than 'just in time' (Frigols et al. 2008: 21). Where language learning is not well integrated into the general school day and wider curriculum, it can only but be a 'bolt on extra' (DfES 2005: 4) and less conducive for learning.

There is a clear need for primary school environments to provide frequent, rich, holistic, real-life, sensory, language learning experiences to stimulate, support and enhance learning. Some primary schools in England have already found ways to integrate foreign language learning into the wider curriculum (Couzens et al. 2013; Schulze 2010). There are already two bilingual English/ Spanish mainstream primary schools in existence (Dupret and Woodhouse 2013). Furthermore, a small-scale case study investigating the impact of teaching French alongside literacy for 7–11-year-olds by Couzens et al. (2013) highlighted a dramatic increase in literacy standards in school; a tantalizing prospect indeed. But in England, such practice currently remains the exception, highlighting a need for considered change.

What other 'everyday' opportunities for pupils to be exposed to hearing and seeing, using and writing foreign languages are afforded by the cultural practices in your school? How meaningful for pupils are the current contexts, and the content, of the languages being learned in your school? Are there ways to better tap into pupils' 'context memories' to improve language learning?

Providing such holistic, sensory, linguistic experiences is arguably not however alien for many schools; indeed school environments provide precisely this for the increasing numbers of pupils with English as an additional language, where such pupils are swiftly immersed into the hegemonic nature and culture of English. Much research abounds as to how quickly such learners can pick up the English language being afforded an immersive learning experience and how teachers can better support their needs in coping with this (NALDIC, online). In seeking ways to better understand and address the needs of these pupils, schools could also find ways to enrich the linguistic environment afforded their monolingual pupils. Currently, there are two separate discourses for foreign language learning and the learning of English as an additional language; perhaps it is now time for these two discourses to 'talk'.

At the end of the day, we are natural beings living in a natural world and so tapping into all things naturalistic should not be too much of an obstacle if we apply ourselves to overcoming the artificial world that is school' (Gilbert 2013: 84).

What could you adapt or adopt in your school and classroom environment to help provide new, challenging, immersive, multisensory, whole-brain and real-life experiences to better support primary school-based foreign language learning, for all learners? (from Gilbert 2013: 126)

References and further reading

Cable, C., Driscoll, P., Mitchell, R., Sing, S., Cremin, T., Earl, J., Eyres, L., Martin, C. and Heins, B. (2010), *Language Learning at Key Stage Two, A Final Report: Department for Children, Schools and Families.* London: Department for Children, Schools and Families (DCSF).

Churches, R. (ed.) (2013), *The Quiet Revolution: Transformational Languages Research by Teaching School Alliances.* CfBT Education Trust.

Couzens, C., Dugmore, J. and Thomas, K. (2013), 'What is the impact of embedding links in Modern Foreign Languages and English teaching and learning across the curriculum in Key Stage Two?', in R. Churches (ed.), *The Quiet Revolution: Transformational Languages Research by Teaching School Alliances.* CfBT Education Trust, 176–81. http://cdn.cfbt.com/~/media/cfbtcorporate/files/research/2013/r-the-quiet-revolution-2013.pdf.

Csizér, K. and Dörnyei, Z. (2005), 'Language learners' motivational profiles and their motivated learning behaviour', *Language Learning*, 55, (4), 613–59.

Department for Education and Schools (DfES) (2002), *Languages for all; Languages for Life, National Strategy for language learning.* London: DfES.

—(2005), *The Key Stage Two Framework for Languages.* London: DfES.

Department of Education (DfE) (2013), *The National Curriculum: Primary Curriculum,* https://www.gov.uk/government/publications/national-curriculum-in-england-primary-curriculum, 193–5 (accessed March 2014).

Driscoll, P. and Frost, D. (1999), *The Teaching of Modern Foreign Languages in the Primary School.* London: Routledge.

Dupret, L. and Woodhouse, R. (2013), 'The development of St Paul's as a bilingual school, with support from the Department of Education and the Spanish Embassy', in R. Churches (ed.), *The Quiet Revolution: Transformational Languages Research by Teaching School Alliances.* CfBT Education Trust, 182–90.

European Centre for Modern Languages, http://www.ecml.at/ (accessed March 2014).

Frigols, M., Marsh, P. and Mehisto, P. (2008), *Uncovering CLIL: Content and Language Integrated Learning.* London: Continuum.

Gilbert, I. (2013), *Essential Motivation in the Classroom* (2nd edn). London: Routledge.

Jones, J. and Maclachlan, A. (2009), *Primary Languages in Practice: A Guide to Teaching and Learning.* Buckingham: Open University Press.

Kirsch, C. (2008), *Teaching Foreign Languages in the Primary School: Principles and Practice.* London: Continuum.

Maynard, S. (2011), *Teaching Foreign Languages in the Primary School.* London: Routledge.

Meighan, R. (2013), 'Mission Control', in I. Gilbert (ed.), *Essential Motivation in the Classroom*. London: Routledge. Chapter 3, 92–121.

National Association for Language Development in the Curriculum (NALDIC), http://www.naldic. org.uk/ (accessed March 2014).

Schulze, V. (2010), 'Integrated Language Learning in the primary curriculum; investigating the impact of a language teaching intervention on teacher, trainee and pupil attitude and motivation; a case-study', http:www.canterbury.ac.uk/CReaTE (accessed March 2014).

Sharpe, K. (1999), 'Modern Foreign Languages in the primary school in England: Some implications for initial teacher training', in P. Driscoll and D. Frost (eds), *The Teaching of Modern Foreign Languages in the Primary School*. London: Routledge, 131–51.

—(2001), *Foreign Languages in the Primary School: The What, Why and How of Early MFL Teaching*. London: Kogan Page.

Tinsley, T. (2013), *Languages: The State of the Nation – Demand and Supply of language Skills in the UK. Summary Report* (The British Academy). London: Alcantara Communications.

Watkins, C. (1999), 'Managing classroom behaviour from research to diagnosis', http://www.academia. edu/547797/Managing_classroom_behaviour_From_research_to_diagnosis (accessed March 2014).

Wray, A. (2008), 'The Puzzle of Language Learning', *Language Teaching*, 41, (2), 253–71.

Should children be learning about climate change?

Stephen Scoffham

15

Children have lots of different ideas about climate change and global warming. 'It is something in Antarctica' said one 9-year-old child when he was asked what he thought. 'The Earth gets really hot and starts to crack,' said another. 'It's when you don't close the door and all the hot air goes out,' declared a third. In just one group of 9-year-old pupils' perceptions of climate change ranged from balanced scientific explanations to egocentric accounts and apocalyptic fears. The child who talked about the Earth 'blowing up in about 30 years' was working in the same class as the pupil who talked about how pollution creates too much carbon dioxide which then heats the atmosphere 'like a blanket'. Some pupils displayed considerable knowledge but a majority exhibited a mixture of confusion and ignorance.

What do the children in your class know about climate change?

It is hardly surprising that children are confused about climate change. Adults are too! The number of climate sceptics had increased enormously over the last decade and there is evidence that around a fifth of the UK population now do not think that climate change is happening at all (Hope 2013). Yet the evidence for climate change is unequivocal. The amount of carbon dioxide in the atmosphere has increased from a background level of around 280 parts per million in 1800 when the Industrial Revolution started to nearly 400 parts per million today. Around the globe, temperatures have risen the best part of one degree centigrade in the past century and they are predicted to rise much further in the years to come (IPCC 2013). Glaciers and ice sheets are retreating in almost every part of the world and unpredictable weather events appear to be becoming more common. In the last 6 months alone (October 2013–March 2014), there has been unusually heavy rainfall in the United Kingdom, a heat-wave in Australia and snow has fallen on the pyramids in Egypt. Meanwhile the drought in California continues.

Have your children noticed any 'extremes' of weather?

Why are scientific knowledge and public perceptions so divergent? One possible reason is that there are powerful vested interests involved and that the oil industry in particular sees global warming as a threat to its business. At the same time there has been a spate of media reports which appear to be designed to cloud and confuse the issues. It is also the case that global warming is an unwelcome message. Reducing carbon emissions involves huge costs and the impact on lifestyles and aspirations is likely to be considerable. Some people are hopeful that technology will come up with solutions. Quick fixes are appealing, particularly if the alternative is to make personal sacrifices. Others are tempted to deny there is a problem in the first place and are deliberately looking the other way. Global warming raises many unsettling questions; exploring them can be a disturbing process.

Discuss what you think about global warming and what is causing it? Can you recall where your ideas came from? How might global warming affect your life both positively and negatively?

It is often assumed that global warming is a scientific problem and that scientists will know the solution. While scientists may be able to explore and explain the processes involved, the challenges presented by global warming require multiple perspectives and involve a range of disciplines. There are also strong political, social, economic and moral dimensions. This suggests it is unlikely there will be simple solutions or definite answers. The web of inter-connections and feedback loops which combine to create global climate, mean that an intervention in one part of the system is bound to have unexpected consequences elsewhere. In such circumstances, the validity of a solution depends not so much on what happens but on who devises it and the criteria against which it is judged. Furthermore, any intervention is liable to have the effect of changing the nature of the problem itself. 'Wicked problems' of this kind are long-term, ill-defined and not testable. They have been contrasted with 'tame problems' which are largely linear in form and susceptible to tests that can be repeated (Rittel and Webber 1974). For many, living with uncertainty is a challenge which is difficult to accept.

Understanding global warming also involves psychological dimensions. The way that we struggle with the complex mix of desires, anxieties, defences and needs which punctuate our lives is reflected in the way that we respond to the environment. Psychodynamic theory draws on ideas developed by Klein, Winnicot and others to explain how we internalize the helplessness which we experience in the first weeks of life. It postulates a number of models such as 'splitting', 'projection' and 'infantile omnipotence' to account for how we become socialized through a prolonged process of careful nurturing. However, in situations of acute anxiety even apparently balanced adults may revert to the strategies that they used as babies. Sander and Conway (2013) suggest that global warming can provoke such anxieties because we know that at some deep level our survival is at stake and that we are dependent on forces that we are unable to control. Furthermore, they speculate that extreme positions, either for or against climate change, show parallels with infantile thinking and the delusion that we can manipulate the forces which threaten to overwhelm us.

Can you think of different examples of denial? Do you think it makes sense to think of climate change in these terms?

The English National Curriculum for primary schools (DfE 2013) is curiously silent on the subject of climate change. There is no explicit mention of it in the Programmes of Studies for science or geography or any other subject for that matter. This reflects a very conscious choice as the government received many submissions on this topic during the consultation process. It would seem that climate change, arguably the meta-narrative of the twenty-first century, is not deemed suitable to be designated as a primary school topic.

Primary school children are well aware that climate change is occurring and they have understandable anxieties about it. Teaching children about what is happening in the world around them can empower pupils and build their capabilities for the future. Alexander's review of the primary curriculum confirms that the children 'want to learn about global warming' (2010: 65) and that 'pessimism turned to hope' where 'schools had decided to replace unfocussed fear by factual information and practical strategies for energy reduction and sustainability' (2010: 189). Similarly, Hicks (2014) sets out a powerful vision of how and why education should be developing positive attitudes and helping young people face the future with as much confidence as possible if they are to discharge their wider role in society. Working together with others, often in practical and participatory learning situations, appears to be particularly effective in promoting positive engagement. A spirit of hope and optimism does not have to be based on bland optimism.

But the argument on teaching children about climate change goes deeper than this. If we accept a commitment to inclusive values, we accept a commitment to the well-being of future generations. It is already apparent that global warming is undermining the quality of lives of millions of people around the world, particularly those who are poor or marginalized. Booth and Ainscow (2010) argue that 'ecological literacy' is, quite simply, the most fundamental aim of education. And they believe that this should grow out of an understanding and respect for nature, out of building our sense of identity and belonging, rather than a fear of catastrophe.

Global climate change is one of a number of pressing problems which have come to the fore in the twenty-first century as the planet comes under increasing strain. The depletion of natural resources, the loss of biodiversity and the degradation of soils and habitats are other examples of what has come to be termed the 'environment crisis'. Yet rather than focusing exclusively on the environment, perhaps we should also be exploring the values that we hold and the narratives which underpin our lives. Lovelock (2007) argues convincingly that nature will always find a balance. The question is whether we will have the wisdom to find ways to live within our means before we irreversibly undermine the planet that supports us.

References and further reading

Alexander, R. (2010), *Children, Their World, Their Education*. London: Routledge.

Booth, T. and Ainscow, M. (2010), *Index for Inclusion*. Bristol: Centre for Studies on Inclusive Education.

Carbon Brief, http://www.carbonbrief.org/ (accessed March 2014).

Department for Education (DfE) (2013), *The National Curriculum in England: Primary Curriculum*, https://www.gov.uk/government/publications/national-curriculum-in-england-primary-curriculum (accessed April 2014).

Hicks, D. (2014), *Educating for Hope in Troubled Times: Climate Change and the Transition to a Post-Carbon Future*. Stoke-on-Trent: Trentham.

Hope, M. (2013), 'Poll appears to show growth in climate skepticism – But what kind is it?', *The Carbon Brief*, http://www.carbonbrief.org/blog/2013/09/poll-appears-to-show-growth-in-climate-skepticism-but-what-kind-is-it/ (accessed April 2014).

Intergovernmental Panel on Climate Change (IPCC) (2013), *Summary for Policy Makers: Fifth assessment Report of the Intergovernmental Panel on Climate Change*. Cambridge: Cambridge University Press.

Lovelock, J. (2007), *The Revenge of Gaia*. London: Penguin.

Rittel, H. and Webber, M. (1974), 'Dilemmas in a general theory of planning', *Policy Sciences*, 4, 155–69.

Sander, J. and Conway, P. (2013), *Psychological Approaches with Sustainable and Global Learning (Think Global Thinkpiece)*. London: Development Education Association.

To explore climate change, environmental issues and the implications for Education in greater depth go to: http://www.canterbury.ac.uk/exploring-sustainability/.

Part III
Using Imagery in Teaching

There is an increasing use of technology in the primary classroom. It is very easy to be seduced by the technical and innovative. This part is short but thought provoking, asking some important questions about the effect of using images in learning. It also reflects on how effective use can be made of this new-found imagery in teaching various subjects.

Is there a smarter way to use digital imagery in your teaching? 16

Karl Bentley

Does this sound familiar? You are sitting in a lecture theatre and even though you find the topic being discussed fairly interesting you just cannot focused on the PowerPoint slides and you start to daydream. Or, maybe watching television and an advert comes on; it does not have much text or a lot of voice over but it stays in your mind long after the programme restarts.

What is happening? How was the use of digital imagery more captivating in the advert than in the lecture?

How can understanding some of the theories behind this help you to enhance your use of digital imagery in your teaching? First let us unpick what is going on in both situations. You are being offered information, some of it in textual form, some of it as pictures and the rest via sound. All of this information needs processing and here is the first thing that affects your response; your brain can only cope with a certain amount of information. Sweller (1988) termed this 'cognitive load' and though he was not the first to identify it, his is the name most associated with the process. Basically, you have so much brain power and it is divided between your short-term memory, what (Miller 1956) called your working memory, and your long-term memory or schema. The argument goes that it is your short-term memory that is the limiting factor and though there are disagreements about just how many different ideas you can cope with at any one time, the important concept is that it is limited. The more ideas you try to juggle at any one time increases your cognitive load to the point where you cannot cope with any more, so you may drift off task in an attempt to reduce this load. This is not so with your long-term memory as the schemas or models of the world that you build there are not limited and do not create as much cognitive load when in use.

Does this explanation fit with your own experience and how might it affect children in your class?

Think about anything that you are now fluent in, for example, driving a car. At first it was difficult and took a lot of cognitive effort trying to coordinate all

[va]rious controls, remembering the Highway Code and observing the road [conditi]ons. This is because a lot of your thinking was going on within your [sho]rt-term memory. With practice, it became easier as you built up and [rein]forced all of this in your long-term memory as a schema called driving. So [that] it for an experienced driver that it seems almost automatic. This easing [of cog]nitive load actually allows you to do other things while driving, which [migh]t always be a good thing!

[Can] you identify some of the skills and knowledge your children have established [in long-]term memory?

[Re]searchers such as Paivio (1986) argued that text and pictures are processed [differen]tly but each is used within our minds to represent information within [our lon]g-term memory. For example, as a young child, you might have had in your mind the picture of an elephant, or what an elephant seemed to look like to you long before you could recognize or spell the word elephant. This Dual Coding Theory (DCT) is important for the teacher for a variety of reasons.

In teaching young children we try to ensure that they have the concrete image available to them before they try to access the text. Just think about how we use picture books early on in education. This association of text with concrete objects is one of the foundations of much academic learning. Different languages associate the same object with different texts but the key aspect here is that once that image is connected to the text then using both is requiring the learner to load up their limited, short-term, working memory. Another aspect of this DCT is that images are easier to recall than text (Paivio 1986), but in terms of sequence, text is easier to recall than a series of pictures. Exactly how we move from short- to long-term memory is a current neuroscience research topic.

Within the classroom we tend to rely either upon rote learning, which does not always infer understanding, or we retain knowledge by developing new schemas through the understanding of how things relate to each other or how they function. To secure the retrieval of that long-term memory we have to either ensure a rehearsal of that memory, particularly so for things remembered via rote learning or we have to relate it to other schemas. So, in relationship to our use of digital imagery in the classroom we might consider:

How do we use images and text together initially to create the correct connection?

Once that connection is made, will using both together may be adding unnecessary cognitive load?

If you want to recall, can images be more useful?

For a sequence of information would text enhance recall of that sequence?

Can we connect this new information to previous learning?

There may be other factors involved with adding cognitive load to an individual's brain and it is be worth reviewing Maslow's (1954) hierarchy of needs to indicate other possible influencing factors on concentration.

The next time you are sitting in a lecture theatre and you find yourself drifting away from the presentation just pause and ask:

Are you being asked to process text, images and talk at the same time?

Do the text and images match or is there a disconnection or dissonance between them that is adding to your cognitive load?

In essence, is the text or image redundant?

Can you connect the new knowledge being presented to something else you have learned?

This leads into your own teaching, so that when you are using digital images via interactive whiteboards, iPads/tablets, computers and other devices, you need to consider the same issues referred to above. How much and what type of information are you providing? Is it an effective learning environment? The advances in digital media mean that you have far greater control over the use of images and text than ever before and as always in teaching you need to ask not just how you use digital imagery but why and ultimately, is there a smarter way to use digital imagery in your teaching?

References and further reading

Maslow, A. (1954), *Motivation and Personality*. New York: Harper.

Miller, G. (1956), 'The magical number seven, plus or minus two: Some limits on our capacity for processing information', *Psychological Review*, 63, 81–97.

Paivio, A. (1986), *Mental Representations: A Dual Coding Approach*. Oxford: Oxford University Press.

Sweller, J. (1988), 'Cognitive load during problem solving: Effects on learning', *Cognitive Science*, 12, (2), 257–85.

How can 'seeing', 'knowing' and 'believing' impact on learning in art and design?

17

Peter Gregory

Have you ever stopped to consider the reasons why the subject of art and design is taught in primary schools? As one of the foundation curriculum subjects, it is quite easy to form the opinion that it is not seen as very important – as was noted by Dyson even in 1989. This view often compounds the challenges that cause some teachers to avoid teaching it in order to concentrate on other subjects by which the 'success' of the school might be measured. The importance of the subject to the creative industries and wealth generation for the nation is perhaps better appreciated in secondary schools and beyond, yet still influences our work at the primary level.

What do you see as the justifications for teaching art and design in primary school?

This chapter is going to focus attention on three important strands of the subject and pose some questions for us as primary teachers: 'seeing', 'knowing' and 'believing'. The first of these allows us to consider what might be gained by being taught to look, that is, actually learning to see. An earlier edition of the National Curriculum for Art and Design contained an interesting quote from the artist and illustrator Quentin Blake (who at that time of publication was the Children's Laureate); 'Art and design is not just a subject to learn, but an activity that you can practise: with your hands, your eyes, your whole personality' (DfEE 1999: 116). Blake held the view that many artists would argue that the subject allows scope for learning to use our eyes well and apply and incorporate this skill in developing art works of our own. In this way, recognition and description can be developed into forms of communication, expression, illustrating, making and recording (Rubens and Newland 1989). The real challenge for most teachers is that they are expected to do something that they themselves have not been taught.

Edwards, an American art educator recognized this and devised a series of perceptions to aid and support her adult learners as they attempted to improve. You might be surprised to learn that she called these 'the global skill of drawing'

(Edwards 1999: xviii). She outlined the aspects of 'looking', that we can master, in a simple way and thereby build our repertoire of perceptions.

Edwards said that this can be done by deliberately looking carefully at a single or group of objects, first at the edges, then the spaces between them and also the relationships between parts of the whole (noting the relative positions between the shapes, sizes, etc.). She then suggests the need to notice the light source(s) and the resulting shadows before considering all this information as the 'gestalt' or the sense of the overall form of our visual study. We should note, however, that she believed that all of these steps are best explored in turn before picking up a pencil or other drawing implement. Over time, people, whether children or adults can then refine their observational skills. This was summed up by a primary-aged pupil overheard in a classroom by Rubens and Newlands (1989: 6) who said, 'The more I draw, the more I see'.

The same principle is used by many others as well. Brice-Heath and Wolf (2004) concluded from a study in a Kent primary school that children benefit from focusing on the details that they see by:

developing 'greater capacity for metaphorical language' (p. 9)
'beginning to practise vital habits of mind' (p. 10)
gaining 'practice in holding attention' (p. 12)
constructing further reminders 'to look again' (p. 16)
increasing confidence to tackle more challenges in drawing (p. 21)
recognising the value of what can be seen – as well as what cannot (p. 23)

Hickman (2005) demonstrated that such foundations could allow significant skills to be acquired later as well as applying 'aesthetic perception' in subtle and technical ways. Barbe-Gall (2005, 2012) emphasizes the importance of talk throughout the processes of looking and creating. Sadly, many teachers are not aware of the importance of these processes and focus their energy only on the final product or outcome (Gregory 2005, 2013).

What then can be known through art and design?

Individuals who possess the richness of experiences referred to above will enthuse about aspects of art – whether basing comments on the language of the subject, sometimes referred to as the visual and tactile elements such as colour, texture, shape, form etc. as indicated in the National Curriculum content (DfE 2013), or about the underlying concepts, composition or techniques which have been applied.

In short, the subject can open possibilities and allow significant connections to be made between areas of learning, experiences or factual information

(Adams and Baynes 2003). This 'knowing' can support art itself and other areas of learning.

From your observations, how has art and design knowledge supported other area of learning? How has depth of knowledge of art or design affected the learning outcomes of work in your classroom?

Sedgwick and Sedgwick (1996: 16) made a series of claims about the subject's potential to aid learning about ourselves, the world around us (including other people), the nature of art itself, the materials and techniques used in making art as well as the development of ideas and thinking. Ofsted (2009) reinforced this view but noted the limitations placed on these forms of learning through art and design and suggested that more professional development was needed for teachers to allow them to recognize the potential for learning. Her Majesty's Inspector (HMI) Ian Middleton (2011) also stressed the importance of learning through looking.

Where does belief fit into art and design? How would this affect your teaching?

The use of the term 'belief' with regard to art and design might seem a strange choice but it is deliberately chosen here as it implies a degree of uncertainty and the need for experimentation. In classrooms where processes are highly valued it can grow pupils' confidence and self-belief which both empowers and develops further exploratory risk-taking (Mindel 2007). To be able to explore might mean, for example, using materials or colours without being sure of the outcome. The construction of the understanding and knowledge so gained will be beneficial in boosting the pupil's confidence for the next opportunity to attempt another unknown in future lessons.

There is an important aspect to put into this learning scenario: the teacher. If you think back of your own experiences of learning in the subject, you may find that you are able to locate the beliefs of the teacher(s) as well as your own. Student teachers often recount their own negative experiences with teachers who stated, demonstrated or insisted on particular outcomes, without necessarily providing the guidance, knowledge or providing opportunities for exploration. Such teachers, it could be argued, had significant and often long-term influence over the learning of their pupils. For those who enter the teaching profession, it is important that they realize that there are other ways of approaching learning. To be encouraged to 'fail without retort' (DfEE 1999: 116) is something which is both liberating and creatively desirable (McGill et al. 2007). Yet even today too many teachers themselves have had insufficient experience of this kind and sadly close down creative opportunities and reinforce the drive for 'reproducing' illustrations or other artefacts (Gregory 2005).

What is your own past experience and how can you offer a more creative and exploratory classroom?

Life in today's society incorporates complex forms of visual literacy and tomorrow's probably even more so. For example, primary school pupils already have access to powerful cameras in their phones and other devises which can significantly contribute to learning. Teachers, and subsequently pupils, would benefit and gain confidence from a greater understanding of composition, use of lighting, colour, and so on in a range of contexts. By adopting the exploratory approach to learning referred to above, teachers could extend their own understanding as well as allow their pupils to explore the subject to greater depths.

References and further reading

Adams, E. and Baynes, K. (2003), *Drawing on Experience*. London: Campaign for Drawing.

Barbe-Gall, F. (2005), *How to Talk to Children about Art*. London: Frances Lincoln.

—(2012), *How to Talk to Children about Modern Art*. London: Frances Lincoln.

Bowden, J., Ogier, S. and Gregory, P. (2013), *The Art and Design Primary Coordinator's Handbook*. London: Collins.

Brice-Heath, S. and Wolf, S. (2004), *Art is All About Looking: Drawing and Detail*. London: Creative Partnerships.

Department for Education and Employment (DfEE) (1999), *The National Curriculum: Handbook for Primary Teachers in England*. London: DfEE.

Department for Education (DfE) (2013), *The National Curriculum in England: Key Stages 1 and 2 Framework Document*. London: DfE.

Dyson, A. (ed.) (1989), *Looking, Making and Learning: Art and Design in the Primary School*. London: Institute of Education.

Edwards, B. (1999), *Drawing on the Right Side of the Brain* (3rd edn). New York: Penguin Putnam.

Edwards, J. (2013), *Teaching Primary Art*. Harlow: Pearson.

Gregory, P. (2005), 'A deserved experience?' *Journal of European Teacher Education Network (JETEN)*, 1, (2), 15–24.

—(2013), 'Should children be learning to make art or learning through art?', in M. Sangster (ed.), *Developing Teacher Expertise: Exploring Key Issues in Primary Practice*. London: Bloomsbury, 87–90.

Hickman, R. (2005), *Why We Make Art and Why it is Taught*. Bristol: Intellect.

McGill, C., Guessan, T. and Rosen, M. (eds) (2007), *Exploring Creative Learning*. Stoke on Trent: Trentham.

Middleton, I. (2011), 'Learning through looking', *AD*, 2, 4–6.

Mindel, C. (2007), *Creative Environments for Art, Craft and Design Teaching in the 21st Century*. London: University of Greenwich.

Ofsted (2009), *Drawing Together: Art, Craft and Design in Schools (2005-8)*. London: Ofsted.

Rubens, M. and Newland, M. (1989), *A Tool For Learning*. Ipswich: Direct Experience.

Sangster, M. (ed.) (2013), *Developing Teacher Expertise: Exploring Key Issues in Primary Practice*. London: Bloomsbury.

Sedgwick, D. and Sedgwick, F. (1996), *Art Across the Curriculum*. London: Hodder and Stoughton.

[To aid your own development, you might like to use an audit tool (in for example Edwards 2013 or Bowden et al. 2013) to strengthen your reflection on your own experiences and the attitudes which may be linked to them. Hopefully, you will be able to find ways to extend your own ways of seeing and apply them to the learning situations which you construct and allow in your classrooms.]

How might the iPad encourage risk taking in the pursuit of artistic endeavour?

18

Claire Hewlett and Claire March

Much has been written about 'product versus process' in relation to the teaching of art and design (Clement and Tarr 1992; Prentice 2003; Gregory 2013). Children are rarely given the time to fully explore and develop skills and ideas in purposeful and original ways. If we want children to learn to think and work like artists, then it is important that we are aware of what this involves. We need to ask ourselves what is it that artists are actually doing when they make art.

Imagine you were asked to draw or paint a picture, how would you start? What would you decide to draw or paint? What tools and resources might you choose to work with? What personal experiences might you draw upon as you make these decisions?

Artists spend time acquiring the necessary knowledge and technical skills needed to work with materials (Eisner 2002) and then use their knowledge and skills in purposeful and original ways to represent and communicate ideas. Mace and Ward (2002) identified what they believe to be the four main phases involved in making an art work. Starting with the initial conception of an idea, this is then developed and refined, leading to the creating of the artwork and finally, phase four, the completion of the art work. Within each phase, the decision-making process makes simultaneous multiple emotive demands of the brain; exploration, experimentation, risk taking, discovery, problem solving, and continuous re-evaluation as the initial idea is further refined. Not all ideas culminate in a successful piece of art work; a piece can be rejected at any stage for a variety of reasons and frequently will be. Making art, therefore, is also about attitude. Engaging with the physical and mental processes identified above requires a certain amount of determination, perseverance and resolve, among other things. When we think about what we mean by 'artistic endeavour' we believe it involves engaging with a combination of all of the above.

How might iPad technology help children engage with and become aware of these processes?

Digital technologies such as the iPad or tablet present children with new ways of engaging with both the physical and mental processes of making art. Stylus-driven drawing and painting programs, enable drawing actions to be made directly onto a screen. Apps such as Artrage (www.artrage.com) are pressure sensitive and marks made with a stylus or finger mimic some of the physical properties and fluidity of a range of drawing and painting tools such as brushes, palette knife, pastels, pen and pencil. Children are able to select from a seemingly endless spectrum of luminous colour, far beyond what can easily be produced by traditional pigments, and re-create an exciting range of effects such as water colour or oil paint.

The iPad enables children to quickly access the tools they need, allowing them to work at speed and with greater spontaneity than when working with more traditional methods (Berry 2013; Wood 2004). Children can respond in an instant to an idea; what would happen if I did this or tried that? The undo button empowers children, giving them the freedom to make mistakes and take risks. Mistakes can be quickly and easily rectified which often leads to bolder experimentation. It becomes possible to begin exploring and experimenting with little provisional planning, allowing ideas to be tested and develop more organically. Work can be electronically stored at any stage allowing children time to step away from a piece and return to it later. How often do they have this opportunity when working with other art forms? Layering allows children to be adventurous and experiment even further with different effects and colour being added to existing work often results in happy accidents. The iPad enables the 'process of constructing meaning [to be] clearly visual' (Buckingham, 167) which allows the children to engage in 'visual thinking' (ibid., 168) in the manner of the artist.

How might you use the iPad to develop art in school?

To illustrate a possible approach we describe a series of lessons which took place with a class of 10- and 11-year-olds. They were involved in a painting project based around the theme of 'water'. Though familiar with iPad technology, the class had not used the devices for art and design. In order to generate some initial ideas, the class were introduced to images of water produced by well-known artists. These intentionally included both male and female artists, past and present, and from different cultural backgrounds. The children were invited to critique the images before using their iPads to undertake their own research, to select and save images they found interesting; this generated discussion and further ideas.

The class were introduced to the Artrage app and, due to the intuitive nature of the iPad, were quickly able to engage with the visual interface. Time was allowed for exploration and experimentation and the children were motivated to explore colour mixing and a range of visual effects. Alongside working on the iPad the class were introduced first to watercolour and then acrylic paint and shown some simple application skills. Again, time was allowed for experimentation and the observation of the effects of paint on paper.

Over several weeks, the children were supported in developing their ideas and had the freedom to choose whether to work in paint or on the iPad. This element of choice was highly motivating and spurred the children on to become quite playful and imaginative in the decisions they ultimately made. Using the iPads also meant the children could photograph or save their work at each stage, another valuable part of the decision-making process, enabling the children to revise and reassess their work as they worked towards their final pieces.

How might using iPads support the development of other forms of art and design in school?

There is an argument that digital art that relies on programs such as Brushes and Artrage merely reproduces banality (Briggs and Blythe 2012) and that it only allows for the simulation of traditional art forms. But why bother to draw comparisons in this way? It is a different art form and should be judged on its own merits. Digital art programs bring their own sensuality to the process of making art. Why should not the 'frictionless skidding' of the electronic luminous paint moving across the glass screen (Matthews and Seow 2007: 256) be just as pleasing as the feel of paint being dripped and spread onto canvas? We would advocate that children should work with both traditional and digital methods alongside one another, as in the example above. In this way, children can explore the mental and physical processes of a wide range of art making as part of the learning process and maybe, as Matthews and Seow believe, technological devices such as iPad art may well rejuvenate rather than replace the act of making art.

References and further reading

Artage, www.artrage.com (program) (accessed April 2014).

Berry, M. (2013), *Creating a New Curriculum*, www.teachprimary.com/learningresources/view/creating-a-new-curriculum.

Briggs, J. and Blythe, M. (2012), 'Post Anxiety Art: Economies and cultures of digital painting', *Proceedings of the 3rd Computer Art Congress*. Europa, Paris, 161–8.

Buckingham, D. (2007), *Beyond Technology: Children's Learning in the Age of Digital Culture*. Cambridge, MA: Polity Press.

Clement, R. and Tarr, E. (1992), *A Year in the Art of a Primary School*. Corsham: NSEAD.

Eisner, E. (2002), *The Arts and the Creation of Mind*. New Haven and London: Yale University Press.

Gregory, P. (2013), 'Should children be learning to make art or learning through art?', in M. Sangster (ed.), *Developing Teacher Expertise: Exploring Key Issues in Primary Practice*. London: Bloomsbury, 87–90.

Mace, M. and Ward, T. (2002), 'Modelling the Creative Process: A grounded theory analysis of creativity in the domain of art making', *Creativity Research Journal*, 14, (2), 179–82.

Matthews, J. and Seow, P. (2007), 'Electronic Paint: Understanding Children's Representation through their Interactions with Digital Paint', *International Journal of Art and Design Education*, 26, (3), 251–63.

Prentice, R. (2003), 'Changing Places?', in N. Addison and L. Burgess (eds), *Issues in Art and Design Teaching*. London: Routledge Falmer, 32–8.

Sangster, M. (ed.) (2013), *Developing Teacher Expertise: Exploring Key Issues in Primary Practice*. London: Bloomsbury.

Wood, J. (2004), 'Open minds and a sense of adventure: How teachers of art and design approach technology', *International Journal of Art and Design Education*, 23, (2), 179–91.

Can using children's visual literacy help them to learn Religious Education?

Aidan Gillespie

19

It would seem that children are becoming more literate, or at the very least, they are beginning to develop different literacies to keep up with the fast pace of the technological revolution. As adults, most of us would acknowledge that we are less literate in technology than our younger counterparts. However, I would argue that while children demonstrate amazing literacy skills both in the traditional sense as well as in the sense of information technology (IT) and its applications, visual literacy as a tool for interpretation is still at a basic level and in need of nurturing.

The term 'visual literacy' can mean many things but for the purpose of this discussion it can be defined as the ability, 'to discriminate and interpret the visible actions, objects, symbols, natural or man-made, that he encounters in his environment' (Debes 1968) or 'The active reconstruction of past visual experiences with incoming visual messages to obtain meaning' (Sinatra 1986).

For what purposes do you use visual literacy in the classroom and what effect does it have on children's learning?

Learning styles such as visual, auditory and kinaesthetic (VAK) have been one of the many tools which teachers have drawn on since the 1960s and have used as a way of identifying the preferred learning styles of pupils in their classes in order to maximize the learning potential of each individual across a variety of subjects (Sharp et al. 2008). VAK styles can be thought of as a cognitive learning tool used by the teacher to engage children in their learning. VAK models are primarily concerned with the teacher's perception with the ways in which pupils learn rather than the children's ability to grasp new material (Keefe 1982). A visual learning style, one could argue, is cognitive preference towards a particular way of learning rather than a pedagogical tool through which a pupil, guided by a more knowledgeable other, can observe and reflect upon the world. To this latter end visual literacy is a method through which a learner is guided to observe and engage with certain media and to reflect upon their own cultural, social and personal frames of reference and to infer meaning from the experience.

To what extent do teachers teach children how to observe and interpret their observations as opposed to offering visual material?

Using visual literacy as a tool for teaching Religious Education (RE) in the primary classroom leads us into some challenging waters but also well-springs of opportunity and potential.

What objects are worth interpreting in RE?

Religious artefacts take many forms within primary schools but the ones which I would like you to think about are artefacts drawn from recognized religious traditions and prescribed from both the locally agreed RE syllabi as well as the RE Councils suggested framework (2013). These include the six major word religions of Hinduism, Judaism, Buddhism, Christianity, Islam and Sikhism alongside nonreligious systems of belief such as Humanism. Within schools these artefacts are replicas of objects used within these traditions.

Alongside of this, objects which share either physical, symbolic or functional parallels to the religious artefacts being used but are drawn from within the pupils own cultural and personal frames of reference may also be included. What is important to note is that it is the symbolic meaning of the object, whether religious or nonreligious, which is important. An object is symbolic to a person if it is imbued with meaning (Lowdnes 2012). For this reason alone, any object can be used to explore RE which contains meaning to either the believer of a particular religious tradition or to the pupil engaged in 'reading' it as a piece of visual literature.

Consider a single artefact. What is its symbolic significance in the light of its religious context?

Pedagogical approaches to RE have over the last 30 years been largely focused on 'Learning about Religion': National Curriculum Attainment Target 1 and 'Learning from Religion': Attainment Target 2 (Grimmitt 1987). Teachers of RE have been accused of an over reliance on the two attainment targets and of misinterpreting what Grimmitt suggested by thinking of RE as a two-sided subject; one side concerned with a personal reflective approach to RE (AT2) and a sociological or phenomenological approach in AT1 (Barnes 2012). Separating RE into two competing rather than complimentary streams negates the possibility of an experience which bridges the gap between a pupil's engagement with religion and a pupil's reflection on it.

One solution to this is to use an approach which uses both aspects of RE harmoniously. Judith Lowdnes (2012) offers us one possible solution and one

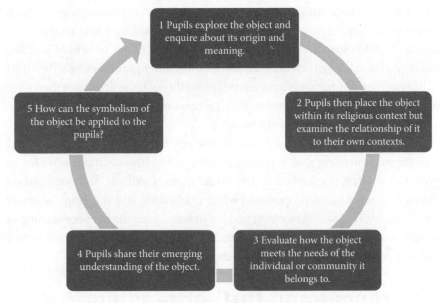

Figure 19.1

which takes full advantage of a child's visual literacy to aid them in their learning. By adapting Lowdnes model to use as a pedagogical tool, we can now explore RE by incorporating aspects of AT1 and AT2 while taking full advantage of the contribution that a child's visual literacy skills can bring to the subject.

As an example of how visual literacy can aid learning, let us introduce a religious artefact for enquiry at Stage 1, perhaps an ornament of the "Aum" symbol within Hinduism. What does this symbol mean to believers and what are the stories behind this symbol? Stage 2 may use visual literacy to contextualize symbols which they are familiar with or that may share conceptual parallels. Stage 3 would be an evaluation of the value of religious symbols to believers and to symbols which are important to them. Following on from this, pupils will be encouraged to communicate their thoughts about the symbols, their meanings to both the believers as well as parallel meanings to the pupil from symbols and artefacts within their own frame of reference (Stage 4). And finally, in Stage 5, we will understand how these symbols affect believers' lives and how the pupils will understand this.

How would you use this staged approach in the classroom? Give an example from your own teaching.

Using this approach we can use visual literacy to aid pupils learning of RE at an age-appropriate level. For younger pupils, using religious artefacts for their physical similarities to objects in their own lives may be one way in which younger children can access RE. Examining an altar within Christianity, could lead to a child's association of it with a table from home or school and the different contexts in which they are used. Or for older pupils, using a Buddhist "Thangka" to draw parallels between devotion through the display of the image of the Buddha to an engagement with pictures of figures important to them and the positive attributes they possess.

Encouraging teachers and pupils to use any tools at their disposal to aid learning is something that is taken for granted but like all things obvious its potential is often overlooked. Using visual literacy skills is just one method through which RE can be explored while celebrating and utilizing the many assets children possess. Assisting children in unpacking the deeper meaning of images and objects from the sacred and secular, religious and commonplace will help make RE more relevant and engaging for them.

References and further reading

Arizpe, E. and Styles, M. (2003), *Children Reading Pictures, Interpreting Visual Texts*. London: Routledge Falmer.

Barnes, L. (2012), *Debates in Religious Education*. London: Routledge Falmer.

Debes, J. (1968), Arizpe, E. and Styles, M. (2003), *Children Reading Pictures, Interpreting Visual Texts*. London: Routledge Falmer.

Department for Education (DfE) (2014), *The National Curriculum for England and Wales Framework Document*, available at: https://www.gov.uk/government/publications/national-curriculum-in-england-framework-for-key-stages-1-to-4 (accessed March 2014).

Grimmitt, M. (1987), *Religious Education and Human Development: The Relationship between Studying Religions and Personal, Social and Moral Education*. Great Wakering: McCrimmon.

Keefe, J. (ed.) (1982), 'Assessing student learning styles: An overview', *Students Learning Styles and Brain Behaviour*. Reston, West Virginia: National Association of Secondary School Principals.

Lowdnes, J. (2012), *The Complete Multifaith Resource for Primary Religious Education*. Abingdon: Routledge.

Religious Education Council for England and Wales (2013), *A Review of Religious Education in England*, available at: http://religiouseducationcouncil.org.uk/educators (accessed March 2014).

Sharp, J., Bowker, R. and Byrne, J. (2008), 'VAK or VAKuous? Towards the trivialisation of learning and the death of scholarship', *Research Papers in Education 2008*, 23, (3), 293–314.

Sinatra, R. (1986), *Visual Literacy Connections to Thinking, Reading and Writing*. Springfield, IL: Thomas Publishing.

Part IV
Learning from Education in Other Countries

Where does education stand in the 'shrinking world' of the 'global village'? As opportunities increase for teachers to learn from other education systems, what can we take away from this experience? The papers in this part are written by people who have engaged with other education systems and it has left them with questions about their own practice which they have chosen to share with you. Will it alter your own view of primary education and will it alter your own practice in any way?

What can teachers' learn from visiting international settings?

Sue Hammond

20

For many people travel is an important part of life. It beguiles with its suggestions of fresh opportunities, meeting new people, experiencing a different climate, stunning scenery and exciting historical or cultural artefacts. More specifically, it has been argued that visits by students and teachers to international settings can be 'transformative' (Scoffham and Barnes 2009), but what enables transformation and is it the same for everyone? What learning might occur? For some people going away seems to have little impact beyond relishing the sunshine and yet for others it can indeed be life changing.

How can teacher visits be different to a holiday?

Although the English abroad has frequently been a subject of comedy sketches, it is fair to say that many people do spend precious leisure trips in their own cultural bubble; packing favourite tea-bags rather than trying the local beverages, preferring food that is familiar, only venturing a short distance from the pool, or searching for English-style pubs or newspapers. To avoid this bubble effect, perhaps the first point to consider before any teacher visit is establishing its purpose.

This can vary immensely and can actually be most effective when its detail is developed organically, as a response to those involved and the experiences that occur spontaneously rather than those set in advance. Even allowing for this possibility, there are certain factors and agreed aims that enable teachers to get the most out of their visit. So, whether there are specific intended outcomes or a reasonably open remit, there should be some overall aims, prerequisites and parameters if educational understanding is to occur.

What might these purposes and considerations be?

Being willing to look, listen and learn are important requirements for any visit. If the fundamental purpose is to develop good practice this necessitates openness and sensitivity. Some visits are based on ideas that emerge from comparative education such as the publication of the Programme for International Student Assessment (PISA) results (OECD 2006, 2013) and England's ranking in the international league tables. Educationalists and policy makers have travelled to contrasting countries, including Finland and China, where young people have achieved success in high-stakes comparison tests. It therefore seems sensible that teachers from England should visit and glean new ideas where the results have been more encouraging.

Background reading or informed discussion about the context should provide insight into the strengths of the education system and raise questions. Furthermore, researchers, such as Egan and Field (2009) have argued that it is simplistic to assume that an education policy, a curriculum or pedagogical approach can be transported and have the same effects in another cultural setting. Learning does not occur in a vacuum and there is considerable evidence from socio-cultural theorists, neuroscientists and psychologists (Tronick 1989; Rowsell and Pahl 2007; Trevarthen 2011) indicating that relationships, environment, expectations, attitudes and behaviours are closely intertwined in the process. Indeed, Finland's social and education systems are good examples to consider for, while their children were undoubtedly successful in the 2006 PISA comparisons, the country has an equality that is lacking in England with its multi-tiered, highly competitive educational establishments (Wilkinson and Pickett 2009). Although an individual teacher is unlikely to change widespread inequality, a visit may provide the space to reflect upon how to support children's resilience, identity as learners, and the realization of their ambitions.

Whether collecting good ideas for improving teaching in a specific school or to challenge assumptions about 'effective' pedagogy, an awareness of the various ways in which children experience education has to be either a vital part of the preparatory stage (Martin et al. 2011) or a key responsibility of the leaders during the visit. Change is an essential part of the educational landscape that is both difficult and unnerving. Yet questioning assumptions and being open to new ideas can be enormously rewarding. A good leader will encourage teachers to articulate their experiences and gently probe their views.

What do you think teachers learn from their visits?

There is no easy answer to this question because people are different. We each have our agendas and preconceptions but having the space to rethink or evaluate classroom practice away from the curriculum and our learners can add richness to teaching. It might be through simply observing that children as young as four are independently organizing games with rules; or that worthwhile lessons can be planned in response to the children and environment even when preset objectives, resources or targets are not available (as our Newly Qualified Teachers discovered when teaching in India); or that there are alternative perspectives about knowledge (Andreotti and Souza 2008).

It may be realizing that when your first language is not spoken and there is a genuine commitment to make contact you are able to understand and to communicate through gestures, body language, sounds and movements. This can be recognized through staying at home but a conscious awareness emerges more powerfully when we experience being a member of a minority. In addition, learning some words in the host language is an important way of showing respect and can also provide the building blocks for shared understanding.

Perhaps the most vital lesson may be that we do want to be different and to retain some of the educational variations that make each culture special. At the same time, visits should emphasize the importance of respecting our inter-connectedness and common humanity and the responsibility to care for each other.

References and further reading

Andreotti, V. and Souza, L. (2008), 'Global learning in the knowledge society: Four tools for discussion', *International Journal of Development Education Research and Global Education*, 31, 7–12.

Egan, J. and Field, M. (2009), *Education Across Borders: Politics, Policy and Legislative Action*. Japan: Springer.

Martin, F., Griffiths, H., Raja, L. and Sibedeh, L. (2011), *Global Partnerships as Sites for Mutual Learning* (Interim Research Project Report). Economic and Social Research Council and University of Exeter.

Organization for Economic Co-operation and Development (OECD) (2006), The Programme for International Student Assessment (PISA), Ministry of Education and Culture, Finland minedu.fi (accessed February 2014) [Finland was1st of the OECD countries In Scientific Literacy and Mathematical Literacy, 2nd in Reading Literacy].

—(2013), The Programme for International Student Assessment (PISA), 'Pisa tests: UK stagnates as Shanghai tops league table', http://www.bbc.co.uk/news/education-25187997 (accessed February 2014) [Shanghai in China was 1st in the OECD PISA 2006 results in Maths, Reading and Science].

Rowsell, J. and Pahl, K. (2007), 'Sedimented identities in texts: Instances of practice', *Reading Research Quarterly*, 42, (3), 388–404.

Scoffham, S. and Barnes, J. (2009), 'Transformational experiences and deep learning', *Journal of Education for Teaching*, 35, (3), 257–70.

Trevarthen, C. (2011), 'What is it like to be a person who knows nothing? Defining the active intersubjective mind of a newborn human being', *Infant and Child Development*, 20, (1), 119–35.

Tronick, E. (1989), 'Emotions and Emotional Communication in Infants', *American Psychologist*, 44, (2), 112–19.

Wilkinson, R. and Pickett, K. (2009), *The Spirit Level*. London: Penguin Books.

Does an international placement develop teacher identity?

21

Anthony Clarke

How often do you hear the comment, 'If only I had the time to go and experience something different'? We feel challenged by the pressures of our professional lives which can be dominated by the demands of government policy and an ever-changing curriculum. We often forget about the wider opportunities available to us. One such opportunity could be an international teaching placement. Teachers and student teachers who have taught abroad often remark on 'life-changing experiences' and how such opportunities can contribute greatly to their personal and professional development. In short, they mention they become better practitioners through observing and engaging within an international teaching setting.

There are several well-documented international teaching initiatives such as the British Council funded English Teaching Assistant placements and Comenius and Erasmus projects. Universities and Higher Education Institutions may also offer international placements as part of a teacher training course either to enhance existing language skills or to observe teaching practices in international settings. Within an ever-expanding global community and a pressing need for pupils to develop their linguistic and cultural awareness such opportunities can provide teachers with the skills and knowledge to meet those needs.

What would you consider to be the benefits of going on an international placement?

One clear benefit is the development of your own personal identity. One definition of identity is the process by which the person seeks to integrate his various statuses and roles, as well as his diverse experiences, into a coherent of self (Epstein 1978). Initially there can be confusion and anxiety associated with a placement abroad and that feeling of being out of your comfort zone. There are cultural and linguistic challenges and a need to adapt to the food, climate or even the classroom culture. However, it is by facing such challenges that you discover your identity and learn to develop qualities of resilience and perseverance.

Can you remember an occasion when you faced a considerable challenge? What helped you overcome that challenge? What personal qualities did you draw on?

Quite often you only discover more about your inner qualities when faced with a situation that is challenging or alien. One such challenge often encountered by both teachers and students abroad is an apparent lack of resources within the classroom. On a teaching placement in an Indian Secondary school student teachers did not have the usual access to an interactive whiteboard to present a lesson on aspects of British culture. Ultimately they drew on their own personal resources to teach the lesson. They used their voices, physical gestures and drawings to communicate meaning. The follow-up discussion revealed how they were previously too reliant on technology and that they had actually enjoyed teaching without the usual more technical aids. They drew on their inner strengths which in their words they 'did not know they possessed'.

What would it be like to deliver a lesson that involved little or no use of technology or resources?

This growth of resilience during an international placement contributes greatly to a teacher's professional identity. Teachers will face professional challenges in a classroom where expectations and routines may differ from an English classroom. It is how teachers respond to these changes which determine how much can be gained from such an experience. Professional identity implies both a cognitive psychological and sociological perspective; through the interactions with other cultures and systems there is that opportunity to develop that perception of who you are and who you want to become (Beijaard 2006). By observing education practice in other countries there is an invaluable opportunity to identify strengths and teaching strategies which can meaningfully inform your own practice. Ofsted (2008: 4) reviewing a bilateral exchange programme in 2008 noted that 'students gain significantly as a result of experiences abroad . . . working in two educational cultures enhances students' ability to reflect on and develop their practice, and mentors on their final placement praised the exceptional maturity of these students'.

What kind of differences do you think you may observe between international and UK school systems?

The international placement can also develop a cultural and intercultural awareness which may involve a questioning of your own national culturally determined assumptions. There is no doubt that it is difficult not to compare different education and cultural systems and one of the challenges is to try and avoid being too judgemental. Each setting has a unique set of values and beliefs which work well within that context. To fully appreciate an international experience one needs to develop a critical cultural awareness but also to be able to 'decentre'. This involves the ability to accept other cultures and to take on a different cultural perspective. Byram and Doyé (1999) refer to this as 'savoir s' engager'; an engagement and an immersion within that culture from which you can reap the full benefits. This intercultural journey requires a dismissal of prejudices and preconceptions and an acceptance that there are differences which will inform your knowledge and understanding.

Can you think of an occasion in your life that has transformed your thinking?

Finally, we consider the idea of an international placement as a 'transformative experience' (Barnes and Scoffham 2009). This transformation begins with a disorientating dilemma which may lead adults to experience a 'perspective transformation'. In short, this can be described as a shifting of our world view in order to accommodate new perspectives. We become critically aware of how and why our own presuppositions have come to constrain how we perceive and understand the world to be. This can be illustrated by a teacher's observation of the use of praise in a Spanish classroom during a teaching placement in Madrid;

> The limited use of praise in Spain made me realise that we tend to overuse praise so much in the UK that it becomes ineffective as a motivational factor.

This 'cognitive dissonance' (Festinger 1957) can challenge our perceptions and expectations which can initially be an unsettling experience. However, this can ultimately transform your identity and help to broaden and deepen your knowledge of alternative teaching settings which can only be beneficial to your future teaching careers.

References and further reading

Barnes, J. and Scoffham, S. (1957), 'Transformational experiences and deep learning: The impact of an intercultural study visit to India on UK initial teacher education students', *Journal of Education for Teaching*, 35, (3), 257–70.

Beijaard, D. (2006), 'Dilemmas and conflicting constraints in teachers' professional identity development', *European Association for Research on Learning and Instruction Special Interest Group*, Professional Learning and Development Conference, Leuven, Belgium, October 2006, Northumbria University.

British Council (2014), *English Language Assistants Abroad*, http://www.britishcouncil.org/languageassistants-ela.htm (accessed March 2014).

Byram, M. and Doyé, P. (1999), 'Intercultural competence and foreign language learning in the primary school', in P. Driscoll and D. Frost (eds), *The Teaching of Modern Foreign Languages in the Primary School*, Chapter 6. London: Routledge.

Comenius Lifelong Learning Programmes (2014), http://www.britishcouncil.org/comenius-programmes.htm (accessed March 2014).

Driscoll, P. and Frost, D. (eds) (1999), *The Teaching of Modern Foreign Languages in the Primary School*. London: Routledge.

Epstein, A. (1978), *Ethos and Identity*. Tavistock: London.

Erasmus Lifelong Learning Programmes (2014), http://www.britishcouncil.org/erasmus-staff-opportunities.htm (accessed March 2014).

Festinger, L. (1957), *A Theory of Cognitive Dissonance*. London: Stanford University Press.

Office for Standards in Education (OFSTED) (2008), *Primary languages in Initial Teacher Training*, Reference No. 070031, p. 4.

International edutourism and voluntourism – who really benefits?

Tony Mahon

22

> I have learned to be a lot more open to different cultures. Before I went I had built up in my mind a stereotype of what I expected the people (in a Muslim country) to be like and I was clearly mistaken.

This is just one of a multitude of reflective comments made by student teachers upon returning from a short-term international placement in another country, in this case Malaysia. As part of its commitment to internationalize its teacher education curriculum, the Department of Primary Education at Canterbury Christ Church University has provided the opportunity for student teachers to undertake a 4-week placement in a variety of international settings since 2008. These placements involve students working in schools or other learning environments to teach English and in some cases other curriculum subjects in a range of countries in Europe, Africa and East Asia as well as the United States. The placements are intended to provide student teachers with opportunities to develop increased cultural knowledge and intercultural understanding, broadened global perspectives and an increased belief in the value of multi-cultural education though interaction with children, other professionals and adults from different cultural backgrounds (Mahon and Cushner 2002).

There is a substantial body of research that provides support for the claim that such opportunities frequently have a positive impact on students' personal and professional development (Cushner and Mahon 2002; Mahon and Cushner 2002; Malewski and Phillion 2008; Willard and Holt 2001). Some researchers have also reported on the transformative nature of such experiences (Scoffham and Barnes 2009). This chapter written by two students, Chloe Lever and Coral Newton, who undertook such a placement at a remote government rural school in Kenya, provides an insightful indication of the nature of the challenges they encountered and the profound impact that they experienced from participating in a challenging short-term international placement.

Although there is evidence of a wide range of potential benefits for the volunteers who participate in short-term international placements, research is inconclusive about the extent and depth of the impact, the factors that contribute towards it, or how long-lasting the impact is (Klooster et al. 2008). In addition, the nature and extent of impact for the participants and communities in the host country is also uncertain; particularly when participants in the host country are from a cultural and linguistic background that is distant from the visiting students. An indication of the complexity involved is provided by Malewski and Phillion (2008), whose research indicated that pre-service teachers' perceptions of members of the host community in Honduras were shaped in quite diverse ways, both positive and negative, by the student teachers' own social class, gender and race.

Key questions arise related to participation in short-term international placements and the extent to which they may be considered beneficial for the host community as well as visiting volunteers. Furthermore, a number of ethical issues arising from such placements need to be considered before reaching a conclusion about who really benefits from edutourism or voluntourism.

Firstly, it is useful to explain briefly the meaning of the terms edutourism and volunteerism. Educational tourism or edutourism involves travel to another country in order primarily to find out about or experience aspects of a different education system. An example of this might be when students spend 4 weeks attending classes at a university in the United States and visit schools where they engage mainly in lesson observation and assisting classroom teachers. Voluntourism implies more active participation and may incorporate a wide range of activities upon travelling to another country to provide some form of voluntary assistance; for example teaching, often for a charity or other worthwhile cause. Many of our placements, particularly in African countries, fall into the category of educational volunteerism. It is also worth pointing out that the word tourism is significant as there is normally also an element of recreational travel involved.

What issues do you think might be involved in international edutourism and voluntourism?

Edutourism and voluntourism have become a million-pound niche travel industry, primarily led by commercial gap-year companies. However, there is increasing criticism of the voluntourism industry by development professionals. One of the key criticisms is that most volunteer placements are too short term and that volunteers tend to lack sufficient cultural knowledge and experience to have real sustainable impact (Simpson 2004). Concerns have also been expressed that the constant flow of volunteers to placement settings such as orphanages can lead to short-lived emotional attachments and a lack of stability for children who are often in vulnerable states (Richter and Norman 2010).

There is a danger that voluntourism can contribute towards perpetuating a dependency culture as schools and charities with few resources become increasingly reliant upon the funding that is received from hosting volunteers. Vudopivec and Jaffe (2011) suggest that this reinforces the dichotomy between wealthy western 'help-givers' and 'needy' beneficiaries.

Our students have found that children in some settings had already formed expectations that the students will provide them with small gifts such as stationery, sweets and stickers. Voelki (2013) found that children had developed strategies to convince volunteers to give them gifts or take them on day trips. She goes on to suggest that children 'conceptualise volunteers from western countries in the light of wealth and giving'.

There is also a risk that inexperienced volunteer teachers may, with good intentions, introduce approaches and methods that are inappropriate for the local context. One example is when a group of our students were asked to teach phonics to children in Ghana in the belief that this would help children to read better. However, after 4 weeks of trying to teach groups of children to recognize letters and articulate unfamiliar sounds, the student teachers left and there was no continuation of the work that had been started. Nevertheless, there are also clear instances where the presence of our student teachers has made a positive impact within a similarly short period of time. In another placement at the same under-privileged children's centre in Ghana, where the cane was used routinely to maintain discipline, students introduced a star chart system of rewards. Children responded positively to this and the system was gradually taken up by the Ghanaian teachers to replace the cane. Several months later, the manager of the centre is proud that the system is still being used by all the teachers at the centre.

Who do you see as really benefiting from edutourism and voluntourism?

On balance, it would seem that there are greater personal and professional benefits for the volunteers than for the teachers and children in the host community. In the case of edutourism, the student teachers benefit from gaining unique first hand insights into the workings of another educational system, which can act as a mirror to help them reflect upon their own values, beliefs and practices. As their involvement in the system is limited, it is difficult to see how they can have much impact other than perhaps challenging or contributing to existing stereotypes. However, when the volunteers are more actively involved, as in teaching and living together in the same environment as the children, the potential impact upon the volunteers can be much greater and can lead to them developing new understandings and skills or questioning deeply their culturally determined values, beliefs and practices. It could also be argued that in some of the placements there is potential for some positive impact to occur in the host community; for example, through children learning about other countries, cultures and language; or simply from engaging in enjoyable learning activities with young people who care about them. However, it must be recognized that in short-term placements, deep sustainable impact is unlikely and there are dangers of unintended negative consequences.

What do you think is the potential for lasting impact?

Ultimately, it could well be the case that the full impact and benefits will not be seen for a number of years and may extend beyond the host community and the student teacher. When the student teachers have graduated and are teaching their own classes, it is then that their enhanced global perspective, respect for other cultures, understanding of the challenges faced by children who are learning English as an additional language, underlying values and beliefs, as well as personal qualities like resilience and flexibility – all of which have been shaped by their international experience, can coalesce to influence the ethos of their own classrooms and the global values and attitudes that are promoted in the future generations of children whom they teach.

References and further reading

Cushner, K. and Mahon, J. (2002), 'Overseas Student Teaching: Affecting personal, professional, and global competencies in an age of globalization', *Journal of Studies in International Education*, 6, 44–58.

Klooster, E., Wijk, J., Go, F. and Rekom, J. (2008), 'Educational travel: The overseas internship', *Annals of Tourism Research*, 35, (3), 690–711.

Mahon, J. and Cushner, K. (2002), 'The overseas student teaching experience: Creating optimal culture learning', *Multicultural Perspectives*, 4, (3), 3–8.

Malewski, E. and Phillion, J. (2008), 'International field experiences: The impact of class, gender and race on the perceptions and experiences of pre-service teachers', *Teaching and Teacher Education*, 25, 52–60.

Richter, L. and Norman, A. (2010), 'AIDS orphan tourism: A threat to young children in residential care', *Vulnerable Children and Youth Studies*, 5, (3), 217–29.

Scoffham, S. and Barnes, J. (2009), 'Transformational experiences and deep learning: The impact of an intercultural study visit to India on UK initial teacher education students', *Journal of Education for Teaching*, 35, (3), 257–70.

Simpson, K. (2004), '"Doing development": The gap year, volunteer tourists and a popular practice of development', *Journal of International Development*, 16, 681–92.

Voelki, H. (2013), 'The experience of children with international volunteer tourists: A case study in an orphanage in Ghana', http://www.voluntourism.org, (accessed March 2014).

Vudopivec, B. and Jaffe, R. (2011), 'Save the world in a week: Volunteer tourism and development', *European Journal of Development Research*, 23, (1), 111–28.

Willard-Holt, C. (2001), 'The impact of a short-term international experience for pre-service teachers', *Teaching and Teacher Education*, 17, 505–17.

What can we learn from teaching in a rural government school in Kenya?

23

Chloe Lever and Coral Newton

In knowledge there is understanding; in understanding there is respect; and where there is respect, growth is possible. (Anon)

We are all part of an ever-changing, developing global community and perhaps as educators, we should prepare children for the future and teach them to be productive members of society by understanding and respecting differences from a global perspective (Emert 2008). The reality of living in a global world can sometimes be forgotten (Schneider 2003) and in order to develop a range of qualities as an educator, it could be valuable to participate in training abroad (Cushner and Mahon 2002). As demonstrated by Kissock and Richardson (2010), such opportunities to teach overseas can contribute to a teacher's personal and professional development by expanding views on the world and increasing professional competence (Clement and Outlaw 2002).

In April 2013, we spent 1 month teaching in a rural government school in Machakos, Kenya. The main purpose of our visit was to continue a reading programme that encouraged learners with English as an Additional Language (EAL) to read using Systematic Synthetic Phonics (SSP). Our experience in Kenya lasted only for a short period of time; therefore, the impact we made needed to be realistic, relevant and sustainable. Our vision was to work collaboratively with the school to provide them with basic strategies to use in a variety of ways and ultimately, to continue to use in our absence.

What factors do you think influence the transfer of a teaching approach from one country to another?

Our experience in Africa has enabled us to reflect on our ideologies and use theories to inform practice. This chapter looks to acknowledge the strengths of teaching abroad and the fundamental keys to learning that we have acquired.

Aside from discovering the country and cultures of other people, teaching abroad has allowed us to better understand ourselves as individuals by recognizing the peculiarities of our own culture and putting values into perspective. For instance, the assumption was made that by providing more resources, student learning outcomes would improve (Kurdziolek 2011). We were apprehensive about the availability of resources and were very wary of using items of value to them. So, with the help of British schools, we raised money to buy reusable equipment for a range of subject disciplines. These included numeracy and phonics stimuli, quality fiction and non-fiction texts for language comprehension, PE apparatus, art tools and a parachute game. Through experience in British schools, children have appeared to be more engaged and excited to learn through the use of different resources. Influenced by the writing of Piaget (1977) and Williams-Siegfredsen (2007) we believed children were likely to benefit from the opportunity to manipulate real objects or apparatus, as it can bring purpose to their learning and stimulate ideas, which in turn, can impact the progress made.

Regrettably, we expected children in Kenya to react in the same way. However, because the resources were so unfamiliar, children responded with over-excitement, confusion and soon, disengaged with the activity. To overcome this, but not rule it out completely, we wanted to provide the children with familiar resources available to them, such as string, sticks, peapods and sand. In doing so, children began to appreciate the purpose of an object to enhance an idea, and soon we observed children revisiting the activity independently in an informal way, therefore furthering their learning. Waite (2011) states that resources don't need to be fancy or expensive; rather it is important to make best use of what you've got! Mangi (2013) also supports this theory stating that a resource is anything we use in order to meet our needs and subsequently this can be adapted to suit the environment.

What have been the most engaging resources in your classroom? Why do you think that is?

In order to teach effectively in a diverse setting, we also had to consider carefully how to successfully communicate academic knowledge to students with English as an additional language (Capper et al. 2000). This in itself was one of the big challenges we faced, especially with younger students who were still developing language skills in their native tongue. We noted that the main teaching style encompassed the classical humanist ideology, with didactic teaching and rote learning, a concept recently developed by Gove (2012). Alongside this teaching style the children learnt from copying out of texts books and through repetition of information. To begin with, we found this strategy hard to comprehend, previously having held a progressive view of teaching. Subsequently, in our own teaching we tried to include opportunities for children to discuss and talk through their ideas based on Mercer's (2000) theory of 'interthinking', which encourages children to gain a deeper understanding through speech (Corden 2000). To scaffold this theory, we pushed tables together in order to create an inclusive, social environment, but to our surprise, due to its unfamiliarity, it led to behaviour difficulties which did not previously exist. On reflection, it is understandable why this approach appeared ineffective. The children were used to following a routine which worked for them, and even though this challenged our own perceptions, it was imperative that in order to continue their learning, these routines needed to be sustained.

To what extent do routines play a part in your classroom and what happens when they are altered?

This experience has taught us to be highly adaptable, self-sufficient, unafraid of risks and resilient to challenge. More importantly, we have learnt to expect the unexpected (Gravells 2008). Every classroom is different; however, nothing could fully prepare us for what we faced. Daily routines seemed haphazard, and teachers would allow a preferred session to be taught, rather than a compulsory one. Similarly, teachers would be absent for long periods of time, whether it was while their classes completed set activities or for little discernable reason. This was so different from what we were used to but we were soon able to develop ideas on the spot, alter plans and generate creative teaching methods using the knowledge that we already had.

Consider a situation where you have had to 'think on your feet'. How have you adapted your practice?

The capacity to manage unavoidable uncertainties was inherent in the realities of teaching in such a diverse setting (Jacques and Hyland 2007). We realized that it was our passion, drive and enthusiasm that enabled us to become more resilient to the challenges presented to us (Warin et al. 2006) and with the support of one another we were able to retain commitment and resilience (Gu and Day 2013).

In summary, we found the whole experience to be rewarding, enlightening, and one that built confidence, thereby enabling us to take with us a new perspective of global learning, to enhance every aspect of our teaching.

References and further reading

Austin, R. (ed.) (2007), *Letting the Outside In: Developing Teaching and Learning Beyond the Early Years Classroom*. Stoke-on-Trent: Trentham Books.

Capper, C., Frattura, E. and Keyes, M. (2000), *Meeting the Needs of Students with All Abilities: How Teachers Go Beyond Inclusion*. California: SAGE Publications.

Clement, M. and Outlaw, M. (2002), 'Student teaching abroad: Learning about teaching, culture, and self', *Kappa Delta Pi Record*, 38, (4), 180–3.

Corden, R. (2000), *Literacy and Learning through Talk – Strategies for the Primary Classroom*. Buckingham: Open University Press.

Cushner, K. and Mahon, J. (Spring 2002), 'Overseas student teaching: Affecting personal, professional, and global competencies in an age of globalization', *Journal of Studies in International Education*, 6, 44–58.

Emert, H. (2008), *Developing Intercultural Competence through Teaching Abroad with Fulbright: Personal Experience and Professional Impact*, http://search.proquest.com/docview/304581885 (accessed June 2013).

Gove, M. (2012), 'Tough exams and learning by rote are the key to success says Michael Gove', *The Guardian*, [online] 14 November 2012, http://www.guardian.co.uk/politics/2012/nov/14/michael-gove-backs-learning-by-rote (accessed June 2013).

Gravells, A. (2008), *Preparing to Teach in the Lifelong Learning Sector* (3rd edn). Exeter: Learning Matters.

Gu, Q. and Day, C. (2013), 'Challenges to teacher resilience: Conditions count', *British Educational Research Journal*, 39, (1), 22–44.

Jacques, K. and Hyland, R. (2007), *Professional Studies: Primary and Early Years* (3rd edn). Exeter: Learning Matters.

Kissock, C. and Richardson, P. (2010), 'Calling for action within the teaching profession: It is time to internationalize teacher education', *Teaching Education*, 21, (1), 89–101.

Kurdziolek, M. (2011), *Classroom Resources and Impact on Learning*. Virginia: State University Press.

Mangi, M. (2013), *The Purpose of Resources*. Machakos: Kyandili Primary School (unpublished conversation, 16 May 2013).

Mercer, N. (2000), *Words and Mind: How We Used Language to Think Together*. London: Routledge.

Piaget, J. (1977), *The Development of Thought: Acquisition of Cognitive Structures*. New York: Viking Penguin.

Schneider, M. (2003), in K. Cushner and J. Mahon (2002) 'Overseas student teaching: Affecting personal, professional, and global competencies in an age of globalization', *Journal of Studies in International Education*, Spring 2002, 6, 44–58.

Waite, S. (2011), *Children Learning Outside the Classroom: From Birth to Eleven*. London: SAGE.

Warin, J., Maddock, M., Pell, A. and Hargreaves, L. (2006), *Resolving Identity Dissonance through Reflexive Practice in Teaching: Reflective Practice – International and Multidisciplinary Perspectives*. [on line] http://www.tandfonline.com/doi/pdf/10.1080/14623940600688670#.U9Y0deNdWvM. Taylor and Francis.

Williams-Siegfredsen, J. (2007), 'Developing pedagogically appropriate practise', in R. Austin (ed.), *Letting the Outside In: Developing Teaching and Learning Beyond the Early Years Classroom*, Chapter 6. Stoke-on-Trent: Trentham Books.

Can the approaches in English teaching be transferred to Indian primary schools?

24

Caroline Tancock

Over the past 20 years, the government in India has attempted pedagogic reforms, including moving towards westernized child-centred teaching, in order to improve the quality of schooling in Indian primary schools. But how far does the Indian government rhetoric translate into the classroom? What is the nature of this change in pedagogy? To what extent is there evidence of the Indian teachers implementing these changes and can English-teaching approaches be transferred to Indian primary schools? These were some of the questions English undergraduate student teachers considered on a study visit to India in 2012.

What is your perception of education in India?

Final year BA (Hons) Primary Education students, who were about to visit schools in the southern Indian state of Kerala, were asked what they thought were the pedagogic principles in Indian primary schools. Here are two typical responses:

> It is didactic, strict and totally different to the UK.

> I think there will be a massive difference in how children learn and what the children learn. I also think teacher ideology will be different to that held by myself and other student teachers.

In pre-colonial India, education was village based and controlled with individualized instructions to small numbers of students. Teachers had autonomy over the selection of the texts and the pace of pedagogy. Central to this was the role of the religious text, particularly of the dominant Hindu religion. The mode of transmission was oral with constant recitation and repetition. These recitals went from teacher to pupil and back again as texts were committed to memory. Underlying all of this was the legacy of gender and caste (Kumar 1991).

Under British colonialism, indigenous teaching continued in many areas but also declined in several others. Macaulay's Minute on Education in 1835 advocated the impossibility of educating all the Indian people, resulting in an educational system intended to create a class of Anglicized Indians to act as cultural intermediaries between the English and Indians. The focus was very much on creating a cultural elite with the purpose of education being used to consolidate power (Scrase 1993).

The period after 1947 saw the Independence movement committed to universalization of basic education but there were differing views of what this meant. For Tagore it meant intellectual autonomy of the 'Enlightenment' and Western Science. For Ghandi it was a rejection of Western Education, However, Nehru held a more pragmatic view, advocating an educational programme which would enable India to engage on equal terms with the West.

In 1986 the National Policy on Education (NPE) stated that free and compulsory education of satisfactory quality should be provided for all children up to 14 years of age. The NPE specified three aspects – universal access and enrolment; universal retention of children up to 14 years of age; and a substantial improvement in the quality of education to enable all children to achieve essential levels of learning. But by 1999, universalization had still not been achieved, perhaps hindered by India's vast cultural, ethnic, religious and linguistic diversity. With this historical background to India's educational system, the English student teachers' perceptions are unsurprising.

However, in the past 20 years, initiatives and official discourses have made references to 'child-centred', 'activity-based' and 'joyful' learning. The District Primary Education Programme (DPEP), which was funded by the World Bank, conducted from 1994 to 2001 and extended to half the districts in India, attempted to transform instructional practices in primary school classrooms through a holistic programme of pedagogical reform. This programme sought to introduce an active child-centred pedagogy in place of the traditional pedagogy of rote learning and memorization (Kaul 2004 in Sriprakash 2009) through changing teaching styles which had previously been associated with low enrolment, retention and achievement in government schools.

But to what extent are these new pedagogies evident and is it possible for child-centred learning to exist in under resourced Indian classrooms? Low income conditions and large classes found in many rural Indian schools place significant demands on teachers. In these conditions, is it not easier to teach with a more didactic, textbook-based approach?

How would you teach a large class with very limited resources?

Our observations of teaching in India suggests that activity-based learning is effective in principle and the Indian practitioners seemed enthusiastic about the effect it has on children's development. However, it is hard to determine whether the application of this in Indian classrooms is fully successful.

> I think the teachers in India are struggling to implement the new approach as it is in stark contrast to the educational traditions that they are used to. The shift in the perception of a teacher also appeared to be difficult to comprehend for the teachers especially those already in the profession as they were moving from an almost dictatorial role to becoming a facilitator. (Student Teacher 2012)

The student teacher above seems to be suggesting that idealized child-centred rhetoric is not necessarily mapping onto the teacher's classroom practices. Perhaps Indian teachers need more support in fully understanding the relationship between activities and learning? The child centred approach to 'activities' seems to have an ambivalent relationship to 'learning' in India as exemplified by some parents, and maybe some teachers, who stated that it was 'playing' rather than 'learning'.

Is this a view held by teachers and parents in our own country's schools?

Sriprakash (2009) suggests that Bernstein's theories of the sociology of pedagogy (2000) can help to illuminate the complexity of pedagogic principles in Indian primary schools and that his views on pedagogic transmission can be used to analyse social control of knowledge acquisition; thus helping us to understand the reshaping of control implied by Indian child-centred pedagogic reforms. Bernstein's theories of 'framing' or 'who controls what' (2000: 12) together with his ideas of visible and invisible pedagogies were devised for Western and specifically the English context; therefore do they apply? Sriprakash's own research undertaken with Indian primary school teachers revealed that the social controls of knowledge remained unchallenged and hidden by the child-centred rhetoric. The teaching we observed in Kerala would suggest that the child-centred and activity-based reforms were not a simple transference of English pedagogy to the Indian context. The lack of resources meant that teachers used themselves as vibrant, creative tools, often reciting stories and poems from memory and engaging in oral storytelling. But they also seemed to revert back to textbook-based work readily in order for the children to be prepared for examinations.

What works in the Western world will not necessarily work in India and perhaps child-centred reforms need to be re-contextualized in order for them to be successful in India. We need to remember Said's (1978) work on Orientalism and remind ourselves that we are observing and writing about India from the standpoint of Western culture, values, politics and economics. We need to be aware of the huge influence of culture on education in India. These changes to pedagogy need to be adapted to suit the culture they are being used in. Clarke (2003) in her study of the impact of the reform process on teacher thinking and classroom practice maintains that the changing of pedagogy is problematic and complex in India. This is because teacher thinking and action is constructed not just through their training but also by the culture that surrounds them. Teachers thus become both 'recipients' and 'sustainers' of culturally defined pedagogical practices. Clarke's study highlights that

> Indian culture and the cultural construction of teaching and learning means changing traditional pedagogy (rote learning and memorisation) is very difficult. (Clarke 2003: 7)

What do you perceive as the main cultural influences on education in your own country?

It seems as if the traditional textbook-based, didactic, rote learning pedagogy is still embedded within the Indian educational system and the cultural dimensions are resistant to change, demonstrating that English teaching approaches cannot easily transfer to Indian primary schools.

References and further reading

Bernstein, B. (2000), *Pedagogy, Symbolic Control and Identity: Theory, Research, Critique*. Lanham, MD: Rowman and Littlefield.

Clarke, P. (2003), 'Culture and classroom reform: The case of the District Primary Education Project, India', *Comparative Education*, 39, (1), 27–44.

District Primary Education Programme (1994), http://www.archive.india.gov.in/sectors/education/index.php?id=14 (accessed April 2014).

Kaul, A. (2004), 'Nali Kali: The Joy of learning', *National Conference on Enhancing Learning in Elementary Schools*. Bangalore, India: Ministry of Human Resource Development and Azim Premji Foundation.

Kumar, K. (1991), *Political Agenda of Education: A Study of Colonialist and Nationalist Idea*. New Delhi: Sage.

Macaulay's Minute on Education (1835), http://www.columbia.edu/itc/mealac/pritchett/00generallinks/ macaulay/txt_minute_education_1835.html (accessed April 2014).

National Policy on Education (1986), http://mhrd.gov.in/sites/upload_files/mhrd/files/NPE86-mod92. pdf (accessed April 2014).

Said, E. (1978), *Orientalism*. Harmondsworth: Penguin.

Scrase, T. (1993), *Image, Ideology and Inequality: Cultural Domination, Hegemony and Schooling in India*. New Delhi and London: Sage.

Sriprakash, A. (2009), 'Joyful learning' in rural Indian primary schools: An analysis of social control in the context of child-centred discourses', *Compare*, 39, (5), 629–41.

What can we learn from comparisons with education in other countries?

Viv Wilson

25

The chapters in this section have examined the potential benefits of experiencing education systems in other parts of the world. Having the opportunity to spend time in classrooms in cultures that are different from our own gives us a chance to reflect on our own values and educational beliefs in ways that can be very positive and leave a lasting impact on our own practice.

However, even if we do not have the opportunity to undertake educational travel ourselves, our classroom practice is still affected by the education systems of other countries in different ways. A previous chapter has referred to the Programme for International Student Assessment (PISA) as one of the international programmes for comparison of school students. Governments in many countries, including our own, take their position in the ranking tables very seriously and become very concerned when they see evidence of 'slippage'.

Are you aware of the international comparative tables such as PISA or TIMSS? Do you know the current position of England in these tables?

These comparative tables have become significant in what have been termed the 'global knowledge wars' (Brown and Lauder 1996) in which countries see education as a vital element of economic success. For example, the results have been used by policy makers to justify educational changes by showing how much better other countries' systems are than those of the home country. More and more often, different countries 'borrow' educational ideas from each other in order to try to keep their place or to get ahead in this international race. The result of this is that, ironically, education policies in many countries are becoming increasingly similar (Ball 1998).

England is no exception to this kind of 'policy borrowing', and there have been a number of examples of the transfer of educational ideas and practices from other parts of the world to this country, although not all of them have been obvious to teachers. One of the best-known recent developments has been that of 'Free Schools' based upon examples from Sweden. The development of the new National Curriculum (DfE 2014) has been influenced by ideas from the United States. Further back in the past, the emphasis on interactive whole-class teaching within the Primary National Strategy (DfES 2006) was influenced by education systems in Asia. Primary mathematics teaching has been influenced by ideas from Eastern Europe and The Netherlands.

Can we 'borrow' educational ideas from other countries and apply them in our own schools and classrooms? Can you identify any difficulties with this?

Looking back at earlier chapters in this section might offer some clues here. National cultures and educational systems can have very different philosophies which affect the ways in which teaching and learning take place. The relationships between teachers and pupils in Asia are very different from those in the United Kingdom, so that the use of whole class teaching did not transfer directly from one context to the other. Conversely, attempts to introduce more group work into South-East Asian schools have met with some challenges (Nguyen et al. 2009).

Direct transfer of educational ideas would thus seem to be very unlikely; even where countries appear on the surface to have similar educational philosophies; there are still cultural differences which will prevent literal borrowing of policies or practices. What happens more often is that educational ideas are translated or reinterpreted in new national contexts, and sometimes are so transformed in this process as to be almost unrecognizable when compared to practice in the country from which the original idea was drawn. One example of this might be the way in which Early Years practice in some settings has been influenced by that of Reggio Emilia in Italy.

The best known example in England is that of the London Borough of Barking and Dagenham which introduced a new approach to mathematics teaching based on practice in Switzerland over an extended period (Ochs 2006). This initiative received national recognition in the early 2000s due to the improvements in mathematics results in Key Stage 2 (11-year-olds). In 1997 the Borough had been among the lowest in the country for results in mathematics when only 54 per cent of 11-year-olds reached the required standard. By 2005 the results had improved by 15 per cent.

So, borrowing ideas from other countries must work then?

The answer here is both 'yes' and 'no'. The changes in Barking and Dagenham took place over more than a decade, and were very systematically developed. Initially teachers did visit schools in Switzerland, but they found as many differences between their experience and those of Swiss teachers as they did similarities. It was clear that they were not going to be able to work in exactly the same way. However, the London teachers liked what they saw, and back in England, the Borough authority developed a pilot programme, supported by professional researchers. This drew on the primary mathematics materials used in Switzerland, but it was constantly evaluated by teachers in order to find out what worked well and what did not. Gradually the Swiss materials were reinterpreted for the English context, until eventually they were effectively transformed and 're-branded' as being unique to Barking and Dagenham (Ochs 2006: 612).

What lessons can we draw from this example?

One simple lesson is that educational ideas from one country rarely if ever fit neatly into another. However, this does not mean that we should reject ideas from elsewhere, because 'they will never work here'. Just as we need to keep open minds as individual visitors to other countries, in order to gain the maximum benefit from our experience, we also need to look carefully at aspects of other education systems which appear to improve children's learning. The first and most important aspect of educational change is that those who actually put it into practice believe it will make a difference to learners. Second, there is no 'quick fix' solution to incorporating ideas from elsewhere into our own systems. Even very good ideas will need to be adjusted to our own national and local contexts, and this process takes time and commitment.

So why should this matter to us as classroom teachers?

Even if we feel we have little or no opportunity to affect educational policy, we do need to maintain an outward looking, curious attitude towards educational ideas. Being able to identify initiatives based upon education systems from elsewhere in the world means that we can investigate the similarities and differences between those systems and our own and make decisions about how best to interpret them for our own classrooms. Rather than being passive recipients of the latest policy directive, we become active interpreters of new ideas to support our children's learning.

References and further reading

Ball, S. (1998), 'Big Policies/Small World: An introduction to international perspectives in education policy', *Comparative Education*, 34, (2), 119–30.

Birrell, G. (2014), 'PISA education rankings are a problem that can't be solved', http://theconversation.com/pisa-education-rankings-are-a-problem-that-cant-be-solved-24933 (accessed April 2014).

Brown, P. and Lauder, H. (1996), 'Education, globalisation and economic development', *Journal of Education Policy*, 11, 1–25.

Department for Education Schools (DfE) (2014), *National Curriculum in England: Framework for Key Stages 1 to 4*, http://www.gov.uk/government/collections/national-curriculum (accessed March 2014).

Department for Education and Skills (DfES) (2006), *Primary National Strategy*. London: Crown copyright, http://www.niched.org/docs/the%20primary%20framework.pdf (accessed March 2014).

Nguyen, P.-M., Elliott, J., Terlouw, C. and Pilot, A. (2009), 'Neocolonialism in education: Cooperative learning in an Asian context', *Comparative Education*, 45, (1), 109–30.

Ochs, K. (2006), 'Cross-national policy borrowing and educational innovation: Improving achievement in the London Borough of Barking and Dagenham', *Oxford Review of Education*, 32, (5), 599–618.

Programme for International Student Assessment (PISA), http://www.oecd-ilibrary.org/sites/factbook-2013-en/10/01/01/index.html?itemId=/content/chapter/factbook-2013-72-en (accessed March 2014).

[PISA tests involve a sample of 15 year old pupils. The 2013 PISA tests rank the United Kingdom overall at the 26th position internationally for mathematics, 23rd for reading and 21st for science. The top-ranking countries in all three subjects were Shanghai, Singapore and Hong Kong. The next PISA tests will be in 2015.]

Trends in international Mathematics and Science Study (TIMSS) (2011), http://timssandpirls.bc.edu/timss2011/international-database.html (accessed March 2014).

[TIMSS results were last published in 2011. Here England was ranked 9th for tests Year 5 pupils and 10th for Year 9 pupils. Fewer countries participate in TIMSS than PISA.]

Part V
Exploring Wider Perspectives on Education

It is a misconception that primary education is a comfortable place to be. It may be comfortable for children but it is certainly not for teachers. There are many tensions pulling teachers this way and that – is research important, can I challenge convention, should teaching be a totally apprentice career, who should I model my practice on? This final part asks some big questions about teachers' beliefs and behaviours.

What's the point of theory? Isn't teaching just a craft?

Vanessa Young

26

Those who know, do. Those who understand, teach. (Anon)

What is your first reaction when you hear the word 'theory'?

Not long ago, a visiting tutor asked my student teachers: 'What is theory?' One student responded, 'It's what they tell you about in university that has no relevance to what you do in school!' Even though it was clearly said out of bravura to raise a laugh, this comment points to a much deeper malaise underlying the relationship that some student teachers have with the notion of theory. It reveals a belief that theory is what professors make up in their 'ivory towers'; something that is irrelevant to practise in 'the real world' of the classroom. Are theory and practice really located separately and respectively in University and School? It seems that this perception is not just held by student teachers; it can also be reinforced by teachers and mentors who sometimes indicate to student teachers that they should 'leave the theory behind' now that they are in the classroom.

Some might argue that there is nothing wrong with this view. Isn't teaching just a craft? The important thing surely is to learn 'what to do' and 'how to do it' in the classroom context. This is indeed the view of the current Secretary of State for Education in England: 'Teaching is a craft and it is best learnt as an apprentice observing a master craftsman or woman' (Gove 2010). The apprenticeship model identified here is indeed the basis for the current policy of teacher training in England (DfE 2010). Increasingly the training of teachers is to become the responsibility of the schools, with the idea that students will learn and be coached by teachers and mentors and have little access to higher education. It is interesting to note that this policy move away from theory runs counter to most of the other European Union countries where teacher training takes place, almost without exception, in universities.

Michael Gove describes teaching as a craft, and at one level, he is right. A craft after all is simply a skill in doing or making something and a craftsman (or woman) is someone who is skilled in that craft. Every professional surely learns the skills associated with best practice from others who have 'been there and done that'. The danger with viewing teaching merely as a craft, however is that it is simply based on pragmatism – what works – without any of the guiding principles, research or thinking that arise from theory. This can be highly problematic. We know that what might work for one teacher, does not necessarily work for another; what works with one class does not necessarily work with another. If what worked in one context cannot be directly applied in another, this model leaves a teacher with nowhere to go.

If teaching is more than just a craft, then what else is it?

We need to decide if teaching is just a craft or if it is actually a profession – 'an occupation, such as law, medicine, or engineering, that requires considerable training and specialized study' (Free Dictionary 2014). While of course it is crucial to learn to be good craftsmen and women from those experienced teachers around us, it is also essential to have a deeper rationale underpinning of what we are doing, going beyond simply 'what to do' and 'how to do it'. For example, you may ask yourself, 'Why is that child so naughty? Why is he always off task?' You may also take it personally. An understanding of the Powell and Tod Conceptual framework for Behaviour for learning (2004) might really help you, not only to analyse his behaviour, but also to know what to do next.

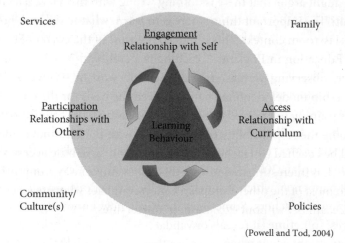

(Powell and Tod, 2004)

Figure 26.1

Is it his relationship with himself that is the problem (emotional)? Perhaps he lacks self esteem or has specific worries. Is it his relationship with the curriculum (cognitive)? Perhaps the task is just too hard or too easy. Is it his relationship with others (social)? Perhaps he is having problems getting on with his peers or is trying hard to impress them. Reflecting on these questions would help you not only to gain insights into the underlying reasons for his behaviour, but most importantly, to address the problems in a way that is likely to be more effective and long-lasting than a mere 'telling off'. A profession sees the importance of this kind of advanced thinking, not just during initial training, but throughout a teacher's career.

I have already mentioned how the current policy in England runs counter to what is happening in most of Europe. It is also interesting to note that the Scottish White Paper (Donaldson 2011), published soon after the English White Paper (DfE 2010) has a different view of learning to be a teacher, arguing that, 'Simply advocating more time in the classroom as a means of preparing teachers for their role is . . . not the answer to creating better teachers' (Donaldson, pp. 4–5). In this policy proposal, Donaldson argues that we should challenge apprenticeship models of work-based learning; 'The values and intellectual challenges which underpin academic study should extend their own scholarship and take them beyond any inclination, however understandable, to want narrow training of immediate and direct relevance to life in the classroom' (p. 6).

How has a theory contributed to your teaching? What would you like to know more about?

Going back to that original question, so what is theory? Theory could be viewed simply as a kind of 'explanation', drawing on the distilled experiences of others. The Greek 'theoria', from which the word theory is derived, meant; looking at, looking more closely, observation, consideration, insight and scientific contemplation. From examining evidence gathered from schools and classrooms, researchers and thinkers look for explanations as to why something might be the case. They draw conclusions from their findings, systematically organizing their ideas and presenting these in a way that helps us to understand (Carlile and Jordan 2005: 4). A theoretical model may even help to predict 'what will happen if' which will help to guide our actions as well as influence our thinking as teachers. Sometimes it reveals new knowledge and suggests alternatives; sometimes it reveals or validates what we already know. A flash of recognition might occur when you see a theoretical model which clarifies and confirms what we've always 'known' or suspected to be true; sometimes, importantly, it challenges and refutes our assumptions and makes us rethink our practice. Theory itself, of course, is there to be challenged and refuted through the exploration of further evidence.

You may think theory is only generated by academics, but all our actions are based on explanations or assumptions which may or may not have been articulated. Kurt Lewin, the seminal theorist famously stated that there is 'nothing as practical as a good theory' (Lewin 1943, cited in Carlile and Jordan 2005: 35). As a practitioner, it is likely that you will base your professional practices on some aspects of theory, however derived (Carlile and Jordan 2005). These may have been developed through your own educational experiences of developing learning strategies with children. You may not be aware of what your theories are; they may never have been challenged, and they may in fact be based on limited or misleading evidence, but they are there. Indeed, sometimes, at moments of crisis, we revert to how we were taught ourselves. You need to recognize when your 'theory' is actually an 'untested assumption' which might actually be misguided. It may also be that during your practice, pragmatism overrides some of the more established, tried and tested theories you have learnt during your training. You may be convinced by Vygotsky's theory (in Wilson and Kendall-Seatter 2010), that children need to talk in order to make meaning in a constructivist context, but at the same time feel that a quiet or even silent classroom is a good classroom. The important thing is to realize this and to reflect upon how you can reconcile theory and practice.

'Theory matters because without it education is just hit and miss' (Webb 1996, cited in Carlile and Jordan 2005, p. 23). Having said this, it is important to stress that the craft of teaching too is vital. Theory cannot be applied, reflected upon and challenged without practice. In the words of Gordon Kirk (2011) of the Universities' Council for the Education of Teachers, 'Teachers without both skills will be a walking disaster'. The relationship between theory and practice should be symbiotic, dynamic and entirely complementary.

References and further reading

Carlile, O. and Jordan, A. (2005), *It Works in Practice, but will it Work in Theory? The Theoretical Underpinnings of Pedagogy*. Higher Education Academy: AISHE, http://www.aishe.org/readings/2005-1/carlile-jordan-it_works_in_practice_but_will_it_work_in_theory.html (accessed April 2014).

Department for Education (DfE) (2010), *The Importance of Teaching: The Schools White Paper*. London: DfE.

Donaldson, G. (2011), *Teaching Scotland's Future*. Edinburgh: The Scottish Government.

Free Dictionary (2014), http://www.thefreedictionary.com/profession (accessed April 2014).

Gove, M. (2010), NCSL Conference speech made by Michael Gove, Secretary of State for Education at *National College Annual Conference*, https://www.gov.uk/government/speeches/michael-gove-to-the-national-college-annual-conference-birmingham (accessed February 2014).

Hulme, M. and Menter, I. (2011), 'South and North – Teacher Education Policy in England and Scotland: A comparative textual analysis', *Scottish Educational Review*, 43, (2), 70–90.

Kirk, G. (2011), 'It's not craft or profession: Teachers without both skills will be a walking disaster', *Times Educational Supplement* (TES), 11 February 2011.

Murray, J. and Wishart, T. (2011), *Teacher Education in Transition: The Changing Landscape across the UK*. ESCalate, http://www.apte.org.uk/documents/2011TeacherEducationInTransitionTheChanging LandscapeAcrossTheUK.pdf (accessed April 14).

Powell, S. and Tod, J. (2004), 'A systematic review of how theories explain learning behaviour in school contexts', *Research Evidence in Education Library*. London: EPPI-Centre, Social Science Research Unit, Institute of Education.

Wilson, V. and Kendall-Seatter, S. (2010), *Developing Professional Practice 7-14*. Pearson Education Limited, http://www.thefreedictionary.com/profession (accessed April 14).

27 Do I really have the time to engage in research?

Paula Stone

> Teaching is a craft and it is best learnt as an apprentice observing a master craftsman or woman. Watching others, and being rigorously observed yourself as you develop, is the best route to acquiring mastery in the classroom. (Gove, NCSL speech, 2010)

Do you agree with this statement? What does this statement suggest about the importance of theory in the teaching profession?

This view of learning to teach places an emphasis on acquiring the relevant experience and using common sense as the key constituents of being a good teacher. This model denies the value of research. Of course, teachers can become better practitioners through the experience of 'making judgments about educationally wise actions' (Winch et al. 2013: 3) and developing their technical knowledge and understanding. However, I would argue that this in itself is not sufficient to be a good teacher. It is through engagement with theory and research that teachers and student teachers are able to form judgements on statistics and policy and its relevance to their practice. Engagement with theory and research can contribute significantly to becoming a critically reflective teacher and this is the one thing that distinguishes the best teachers from others (Winch et al. 2013).

What contribution can educational research make to a teacher's professional competency? Jot down any initial thoughts about this?

An essential part of most university-based teacher education programmes in the United Kingdom is the reflection on action through which the student teacher reflects on what they have done with a view to improving their practice in the future (Schön 1987) and, critically analysing past and current educational theory. However, I would argue that both of these approaches to critical reflection can be enhanced if student teachers and teachers are encouraged to engage in a more systematic approach to research into their own practice. This is not a new idea. Lawrence Stenhouse (1975) was one of the first educationalists to promote the idea of the teacher as 'extended professional' which encompasses 'systematic self-study' and the 'testing of theory in practice' (p. 144).

However, a constant cry from students and teachers alike is, 'How do I find time to engage in research when I am so busy preparing to teach and teaching?' It is not as difficult as it might first appear. Probably the most accessible way to engage in research-based practice is to partake in teacher-enquiry. This is often called 'action research' because the findings are fed back into the original situation to bring about change. As the research is conducted by the teacher/ student teacher it becomes a process that helps the teacher/student teacher to develop a deeper understanding of what they are doing in their everyday practice. It has both a personal and a social aim. The personal aim is the improvement of your own learning and the social aim is the improvement of your own practice and the impact this has on the learners (Mcniff and Whitehead 2010). Thus, teacher-enquiry is a systematic way of examining and improving your practice.

It often begins with something in a teacher's practice that they want to examine and improve upon, so the research process becomes a developmental process of identifying a problematic issue, imagining a possible solution, trying it out, evaluating it and changing practice in the light of the evaluation. Action research begins with the question, 'How do I improve my work?' (Mcniff and Whitehead 2010).

Thus, underpinning action research is a constant evaluation of what you are doing, why you are doing it that way, and the impact this has on teaching and learning. I suggest that action research is not seen as a 'bolt on' or an additional task to complete; it should be part of every teacher's professional development and should be embedded in their practice from the outset and be on-going through their training . . . and beyond. Thus, action research is inspired and sustained by a commitment to educational improvement.

Research literature offers a number of different models for teacher-enquiry/ action research. This model has been adapted from a model developed by McNiff and Whitehead (2010). First, you need to identify something that you are interested in researching. Is there something in your practice you think you could do better? Are you worried about a particular group of learners? You will need to be clear in your own mind about why you want to examine this issue. Is it something that is contrary to your values and beliefs? Action research is often a way of working that helps identify the values and beliefs that are important to us as teachers.

What aspects of your practice that you would like to problematize, improve on, challenge, or are worried about and would like to change?

Once you have identified a research issue, you should formulate a research question. This can be stated in terms of 'How do I . . . ?' These are some of the research questions student teachers, with whom I have worked, have posed:

> How do I use questions more effectively to enhance children's learning in history?
> How can I use guided group work to enhance children's learning in reading?
> How can I use mixed ability groupings to enhance children's engagement with science?
> How can I use assessment more effectively to improve the behaviour in my class?
> How do I encourage 5-year-olds to make mathematical marks?
> How can I use Systematic Synthetic Phonics to help the less able 11-year-olds read?

Can you now write your issue as a 'How can I . . . ?' type of question?

You will then need to think about how you will gather the evidence to show what you are doing is making an impact on children's learning. Write down what evidence you can gather to show your practice is having an impact on children's learning; for example, if you want to examine your use of questioning, you could start by asking a teaching assistant to write down the type of questions you are asking. You could then look at how many open and closed questions you used. You could then try to introduce more open-ended questions. Your teaching assistant could then record how children respond to these types of questions. You can use a variety of methods for collecting this data – journals, diaries, notes, audio and videotape recordings, surveys, attitude scales, pictures, to name a few. Be sure that you are sensitive to any ethical and moral issues that may arise.

Once you have gathered your evidence, you will need to examine the data and evaluate the impact of what you are doing. This may make you consider how you will change or develop your practice. You should continue to evaluate your 'interventions' until you have answered your question.

The final and most important step is to think about how you can share your enquiry with others; this is an important part of educational research. Think about how you could do this with your colleagues and others.

Can you come up with more ideas than I have here?

This could be done through collaborating with colleagues to develop practice across the school. You could perhaps consider using lesson study. This is a form of collaborative practice based on the professional sharing of practice in which a group of teachers collaborate, identifying a research theme that relates to the school's improvement plan. For more details, see Burghes and Robinson (2009). Or, you could share your research by publishing your findings through a subject association or primary teaching magazine such as *The Times Educational Supplement* (TES) or *Teach Primary* or even through a blog (e.g. http://www.consider-ed.org.uk/). Most primary forums would be delighted to receive an example of practitioner-based research that contributes to the growing body of knowledge of what is happening in the primary classroom. Many higher-education institutions offer academic professional development programmes designed to support action research projects for teachers. These would provide you with support from tutors and a group of peers with whom to collaborate and share ideas.

What better reason can one have to engage in action research than to improve your practice for your own benefit and for the benefit of the children in your care, that is, to provide improved opportunities for learning? In addition, if you can improve what you are doing, or at least develop your understanding of what you are doing, this will enable you to articulate good practice and begin influencing the situation you are working in. Furthermore, your increased awareness and your readiness to be self-critical will probably have an influence on your colleagues' practice too.

References and further reading

Burghes, D. and Robinson, D. (2009), *Lesson Study: Enhancing Mathematics Teaching and Learning*. Plymouth: UK Centre for Innovation in Mathematics Teaching (CIMT), http://www.cimt.plymouth.ac.uk/papers/lessonstudy.pdf (accessed February 2014).

McNiff, J. and Whitehead, J. (2010), *You and Your Action Research Project* (3rd edn). London and New York: Routledge.

NCSL (2010), Speech made by Michael Gove, Secretary of State for Education at *National College Annual Conference,* http://www.mantleoftheexpert.com/wp-content/uploads/2010/06/2010-June-17-MGove-NCSL.pdf (accessed February 2014).

Schön, D. (ed.) (1987), 'Teaching artistry through reflection-in-action', in *Educating the Reflective Practitioner*. San Francisco, CA: Jossey-Bass Publishers, 22–40.

Stenhouse, L. (ed.) (1975), 'The teacher as researcher', in *An Introduction to Curriculum Research and Development*. London: Heinemann, 142–65.

Teach Primary Magazine, available at http://www.teachprimary.com/ (accessed March 2014).

Times Educational Supplement (TES), available at http://news.tes.co.uk/ (accessed March 2014).

Winch, C., Oancea, A. and Orchard, J. (2013), 'The contribution of educational research to teachers' professional learning – philosophical understandings', *Paper of British Educational Research Association: Research and Teacher Education*: The BERA-RSA Inquiry (December 2013), http://www.bera.ac.uk/wp-content/uploads/2014/02/BERA-Paper-3-Philosophical-reflections.pdf (accessed January 2014).

Why shouldn't teachers be political? 28
Rebecca Austin and Graham Birrell

There appears to be an assumption that it is wrong for primary school teachers to be political. In recognition of the powerful and influential position that teachers hold and must not abuse, many teachers talk about the importance of neutrality and of avoiding indoctrination of their pupils by sharing their political views. However, we would argue that this is a narrow definition of what 'being political' actually means. It suggests that what teachers should avoid is ideology and views associated with political parties. However, being political is also about understanding the origins and practical incarnation of ideas of political groups; knowing how people are motivated and how their actions are informed by their beliefs; and about understanding the power relationships between different sets of people and the consequence this holds for individuals. We therefore see education as inherently and unavoidably political and all teachers are political whether they recognize it or not.

Do you recognize how you are political?

It is naïve to believe that education is divorced from the political process. At every level from the Secretary of State for Education (in England) downwards there are decisions being made, from who decides the curriculum, to what goes in it, to how it should be taught and in what sort of schools – these are political decisions. This filter should not be ignored by teachers because the decisions taken at every level affect their pedagogy – their very interactions with the children in their class. For example, take the Early Years Foundation Stage (DfE 2012) for 3–5-year-olds: a political decision has been taken about what 5-year-olds in England should be achieving and this inevitably has significant consequences for the teaching approaches taken in nurseries and reception classes (4–5 years) across the country. Foundation Stage teachers will make decisions every day, which are based on politics. Another example is how national tests have narrowed the curriculum to the subjects tested (English, mathematics and science) and forced teachers into teaching for the test rather than focusing on a broad curriculum informed by student need (Stevenson and Wood 2013).

Can teaching ever be a neutral act?

It is possible to argue that teaching in itself is a political act (Kroll et al. 2004). A teacher is in the persuasion business; teachers set out to communicate clearly and they decide (within the restrictions of set curricula) what is most important to know and what is not. They seek to persuade students all the time; for example, in the power of literature; of the beauty of mathematical formulae or of why certain historical events still resonate to this day. All of these examples rest on teachers having beliefs, opinions and in arguing powerfully for them to the extent that young children will believe them too. It is right to believe wholeheartedly and passionately in the things that you are teaching. For example, can you teach about slavery in a neutral, non-political way? Is it acceptable to teach things in ways which you believe to be wrong; would not that call into question your integrity as an educator?

The Brazilian educator, Paulo Freire, wrote that without criticality teachers become agents of a powerful state; in fact, Freire went so far as to argue that educators have a duty to *not* be neutral (Horton and Freire 1990). In Freire's most famous work, *Pedagogy of the Oppressed*, he wrote that when political leaders fail to properly include the people in discussions on the future and 'insist on imposing their decisions, [they] do not organize the people – they manipulate them. They do not liberate, nor are they liberated: they oppress' (Freire 1968: 178). Freire included teachers and education as a vital part of this agenda. For this reason, we would argue, teachers *must* be aware of and question political decision making and its consequences. This doesn't mean they must disagree, it just means they must know why and how the decisions are made.

Can you see this happening in your practice? Are you being asked to make decisions, possibly every day, which are based on politically driven directives?

We argue that there is a three-stage process that all teachers should consider: the first is to simply know that most decisions about education are not taken in a political vacuum and a political process has taken place which has finished with you being asked to teach in a certain way; the second stage is to reflect on this and critique it; and the final stage is to act against it, if appropriate. We are not necessarily arguing that teachers should be political so they can engage in the final stage at *all* times, but if you fail to at least recognize and reflect on how politics is influencing decisions taken at school and classroom level, you have become an unthinking sheep, an agent of the latest pedagogical fashion and in turn a deliverer of other people's agendas. Ironically, in this scenario, you are perhaps being the most political of all as you have been used by the state to further its own political objectives (Foucault 1977). It is perhaps ironic that resistance to government agendas has been deemed 'political' (in its derogatory meaning) as a means to prevent teachers from questioning the will of the state and the educational practices which it deems appropriate.

Being political as a teacher therefore helps you to retain your critical edge and your intellectual integrity. Losing these reduces your humanity and brings you closer towards a robotic state of acquiescent teaching where compliance becomes more important than genuine education. The critical theorist, Henry Giroux, has written about how schools can become 'dead-zones of the imagination' in these scenarios, where critical thinking is not just frowned upon but actively stamped out (Giroux 2013).

Why did you decide to become a teacher?

For some of you this may come under the heading 'social justice' or for others a belief in the transformative power of learning and fulfilling the potential of the next generation. For all, we believe it was a highly positive reason to do with change and making a difference. Fullan argues powerfully that teachers must become change agents 'because systems don't change by themselves' (Fullan 1993: 11). Seeking to improve the present and future lives of children in society *is* political and there is nothing wrong with that. In contrast, does anyone go into teaching to instead be the deliverer of the latest government agenda? But is this the role that many teachers end up adopting? At some stage do teachers forget why they wanted to teach in the first place and simply fall in line with the policies of whatever government happens to be in charge?

The role of government, and therefore of politics, is to make decisions and design policies as to how our lives should be structured and controlled. Education policies set out what all children need to learn in order to be successful and productive citizens. But politicians do not agree with each other, nor do they always agree with educational research (and let's face it, researchers do not always agree with each other either); therefore education policies represent particular beliefs or points of view which support current ideology. They are subject to constant change and to the whim of whichever party is in power, or government minister in charge of education. *You* need to know what *you* believe in because we need teachers to be able to ride political currents and have a pedagogical identity rooted in belief that can last a lifetime in teaching, not just the current trends.

References and further reading

Cochran-Smith, M. (2006), *Policy, Practice, and Politics in Teacher Education: Editorials from the Journal of Teacher Education*. California: Corwin Press.

Department for Education (DfE) (2012), *Early Years Foundation Stage*. London: HMSO.

Foucault, M. (1977), *Discipline & Punish*. London: Random House.

Freire, P. (1968), *Pedagogy of the Oppressed*. Harmondsworth: Penguin.

Fullan, M. (1993), 'Why teachers must become change agents', *Educational Leadership*, 50, (6), 1–13.

Giroux, H. (2013), *When Schools Become Dead Zones of the Imagination: A Critical Pedagogy Manifesto*, available at: http://www.truth-out.org/opinion/item/18133-when-schools-become-dead-zones-of-the-imagination-a-critical-pedagogy-manifesto (accessed 1 April 2014).

Horton, M. and Freire, P. (1990), *We Make the Road by Walking: Conversations on Education and Social Change*. Philadelphia: Temple University Press.

Kroll, L. (2004), *Teaching as Principled Practice: Managing Complexity for Social Justice*. California: Sage.

Stevenson, H. and Wood, P. (2013), 'Markets, managerialism and teachers' work: The invisible hand of high stakes testing in England', *The International Education Journal: Comparative Perspectives*, 12, (1), 42–61.

Should primary education be beyond party politics?

29

Jill Matthews

I read with horror this headline in the *i* newspaper, 'Parents chasing school slots for two-year-olds' (*Independent*, April 2014). The gist of the article was that 'good' schools are so oversubscribed in England that some parents feel the only way to guarantee a place is to enroll their child at the schools' nurseries, effectively creating an expected school starting age of two. *The Telegraph* (April 2014) informed me that 'almost 40 per cent of infants in parts of the country failed to secure places at the main school of their choice' and that, 'hundreds would not be allocated a school place at all'. What is going on? There are several issues here; what is a 'good' school? Why aren't infants able to secure places at their first choice school and why is their first choice school not their local school?

This 'post-code lottery' of finding a 'good' school reflects the socio-economic status of the surrounding area, the number of children attaining high levels in national tests and how many children go on to selective secondary education. Researching the effect of background on attainment in literacy, Kellett (2009: 395) found that children from affluent backgrounds 'exuded literacy confidence derived from a variety of opportunities: routine support for homework, parental dialogue providing good role models, favourable environments for reading and writing, absence of distractions and opportunities to talk about literacy'. Children from poorer backgrounds did not have these opportunities and thus lacked confidence. I contend that this confidence, or lack of it, is reflected across all areas of the curriculum, not just literacy. Yet, schools in areas with high levels of socio-economic deprivation are expected to maintain similar levels of attainment as their more fortunate peers and can be deemed to be failing although rates of progress may be higher. Unemployment, particularly that which has affected generations within a family, and the resulting poverty, impacts on every facet of a child's experience of school. Interventions may plug a gap in the short-term but unless a radical and more comprehensive answer to address these fundamental social issues is found, our

English education system will continue to fail a large proportion of the population (Dyson and Raffo 2007; Horgan 2009). I believe that the current educational policy in England acts to the detriment of all children, but, particularly, to those who bring less of Bourdieu's 'cultural capital' to their schooling (DiMaggio 1982).

What do you think determines a good school?

The introduction of a national curriculum in 1988 was intended to standardize the content taught to all children within England and Wales. This, it was believed, would allow progress in English, mathematics and science to be assessed nationally; it would promote continuity and coherence; it would promote public understanding of the curriculum and provide data which would enable parents to choose which school they wished for their children. However, increasing political influence in the way the curriculum is delivered and the ways in which schools are funded have contributed towards the current status quo. Freire's (1968) proposal of oppression and manipulation appears to have become a reality within the state sector of education, where children's learning is treated as a kind of production line:

child + correct teaching input + correct curriculum → currently at least two or three sub-levels of measured progress per year,

with children becoming mere end products. Since the establishment in 1992 of the Office for Standards in Education (Ofsted), the role of school inspections seems to have moved from one of providing evidence-based independent advice about the effects of government policy on schools to one of regulating and policing primary schools' compliance with national directives. Political party rhetoric regarding 'falling standards' has increased, particularly prior to elections. Schools are under pressure to gain high test scores, which are published in league tables. This can restrict opportunities for effective learning in the classroom because staff, to ensure higher results, may focus more on teaching to the test than on creativity (Turner-Bisset 2007).

How do you create opportunities for effective learning?

Performance in international league tables has been used as a justification for introducing curriculum change, more testing and greater accountability. The media and political rhetoric tends to perpetuate a 'blame culture'. Current publicity regularly comments negatively on the United Kingdom's falling performance of 15-year-olds in the OECD Programme for International Student Assessment (PISA 2012) and draws causal links of this 'fall in standards' directly to weaknesses in teaching and failing schools. One has to ask whether current educational policy in England, which is, by its political nature, short-term, reflecting neither research findings on effective pedagogy and curricula, nor appears to have the philosophical vision and commitment to ameliorate social conditions, is effective?

Not all the participating countries subject their primary education system to the same degree of political control as England. Finland and Switzerland both continue to perform well in international tests (OECD 2013), despite children not starting formal education until they are seven years old, having inclusive education philosophies, a norm of mixed ability classes taught by non-specialist class teachers until the final three years of compulsory schooling and little private sector provision. Standards in these countries are maintained in spite of no national testing until the final year of compulsory education. In both these countries, kindergarten or nursery education is not compulsory. Early years' education is focused on learning social skills, learning to play principally outdoors and to listen attentively to others. The first six years of compulsory education, (7–13 years of age) is focused on social cohesion and the acquisition of basic skills. Children become confident learners. Elliott et al (2001) suggest that 'education reflects the zeitgeist of our rapidly changing times (p. 60)'. At the moment our education system reflects a culture of overwork and lack of work/life balance; it exacerbates the differences between the 'haves and have-nots'. Basic education should be free for all pupils. In addition to free tuition, pupils should receive free learning materials, school meals, school health and dental care and travel to and from school.

What examples can you give of political influence in the way you teach your class?

All children need to be able to access the culture and language of school before they can be successful learners within that environment. I suggest that more time should be spent throughout the whole primary school supporting children's play, both independent and interactive, so that they become socially adjusted to working productively with other children. Both Baines et al. (2009) and Kershner et al. (2014) provide evidence that developing social skills leads to productive learning. By play and playful learning I mean engaging children in activities which are meaningful to them, provide a sufficient degree of intellectual challenge to engross them in 'creative flow' (Csikszentmihalyi 1991) and provide them with a sense of achievement (Papert 1993).

Ideally, primary education should be about instilling a love of learning, creating social cohesion and an atmosphere of mutual respect as well as achieving basic standards of numeracy and literacy. Plowden (1967) suggested that education starts with the child. Can more emphasis be given to creating inclusive schools where every member is valued; to enable all children to engage in creative learning environments where collaborative playful learning is facilitated? Teachers should be encouraged to engage in their own active ongoing professional development and further study but should also be given professional autonomy within the classroom to nurture children as individuals. We should have the confidence to listen to research findings. We should have the confidence to see education as a means of reaching the aspirations we hold for our society. Education should be set beyond the reach of party politics.

References and further reading

Adams, K. (2013), 'Childhood in crisis? Perceptions of 7–11-year-olds on being a child and the implications for education's well-being agenda', *Education 3-13: International Journal of Primary, Elementary and Early Years Education*, 41, (5), 523–37.

Baines, E., Rubie-Davies, C. and Blatchford, P. (2009), 'Improving pupil group work interaction and dialogue in primary classrooms: Results from a year-long intervention study', *Cambridge Journal of Education*, 39, (1), 95–117.

Csikszentmihalyi, M. (1991), *Flow: The Psychology of Optimal Experience*. New York: Harper-Collins Publishing.

DiMaggio, P. (1982), 'Cultural capital and school success: The impact of status culture participation on the grades of U.S. high school students', *American Sociological Review*, 47, (2), 189–201.

Dyson, A. and Raffo, C. (2007), 'Education and disadvantage: The role of community-oriented schools', *Oxford Review of Education*, 33, (3), 297–314.

Education in Switzerland, www.about.ch/education/index.html (accessed April 2014).

Elliott, J., Hufton, N., Illushin, L. and Lauchlan, F. (2001), 'Motivation in the Junior Years: International perspectives on children's attitudes, expectations and behaviour and their relationship to educational achievement', *Oxford Review of Education*, 27, (1), 37–68.

Freire, P. (1968), *Pedagogy of the Oppressed*. Harmondsworth: Penguin.

Horgan, G. (2009), '"That child is smart because he's rich": The impact of poverty on young children's experiences of school', *International Journal of Inclusive Education*, 13, (4), 359–76.

Independent: Garner, R. (2014), 'Parents chasing school slots for two-year-olds', *i Independent* (16 April 2014).

Kellett, M. (2009), 'Children as researchers: What we can learn from them about the impact of poverty on literacy opportunities?', *International Journal of Inclusive Education*, 13, (4), 395–408.

Kershner, R., Warwick, P., Mercer, N. and Kleine-Staarman, J. (2014), 'Primary children's management of themselves and others in collaborative group work: "Sometimes it takes patience . . ."', *Education 3-13: International Journal of Primary, Elementary and Early Years Education*, 42, (2), 201–16.

Organisation for Economic Co-operation and Development (OECD) (2012), *The Programme for International Student Assessment* (PISA) (2012), http://www.minedu.fi/pisa/piirteita.html?lang=en (accessed April 2014).

Papert, S. (1993), *The Children's Machine: Rethinking school in the Age of the Computer*. New York: Basic Books.

The Plowden Report (1967), *Children and their Primary Schools, A Report of the Central Advisory Council for Education (England)*. London: Her Majesty's Stationery Office.

Soler, J. and Miller, L. (2003), 'The struggle for early childhood curricula: A comparison of the English Foundation Stage Curriculum, Te Whäriki and Reggio Emilia', *International Journal of Early Years Education*, 11, (1), 57–68.

The Telegraph (24 April 2014), 'Primary places in short supply', http://www.telegraph.co.uk/education/educationopinion/10770343/Primary-school-places-in-short-supply.html (accessed April 2014).

Turner-Bissett, R. (2007), 'Performativity by stealth: A critique of recent initiatives on creativity', *Education 3-13: International Journal of Primary, Elementary and Early Years Education*, 35, (2), 193–203.

Wilshaw, M. (2014), 'Unsure Start', *Early Years Annual Report 2012-13*, Report launch speech. Church House, Westminster, 14 April 2014, www.ofsted.gov.uk/resources/ofsted-early-years-annual-report-201213-unsure-start-hmci-speech (accessed April 2014).

30 What is the difference between a role model and a mentor?

Peter Dorman

I'd like to tell you a story about a young teacher. I'll call her Anna as this isn't her name. In the final year of her undergraduate programme, Anna, along with the rest of her year group were given a lecture – as it happens, it was on 'Teacher Resilience' but that is not important in this story – what is important is, who gave the lecture and how Anna responded. The lecturer drew heavily on her own recently completed PhD thesis and the lecture was, well, really quite taxing. It was full of references to a French sociologist and Greek mythology and ideas that the students were not familiar with.

Think of a time when you have either read or heard something that was difficult and you felt really detached, and asked yourself what has this got to do with what I have to teach on Monday? How do you account for such feelings?

Now here is the key point in this story. As Anna came out of the lecture theatre she dashed across to me and while other students could be heard stage-muttering how hard the lecture had been and asking what was it all about, said, 'Peter, how great was that. That's what I want to do; I want to be like that, to have things to say and to say them as well'. I assume that you had guessed that this might have been her response. After all, you know how stories work. If you are cynical at all you might now be asking yourself why she responded like that. Here is a non-cynical reading of what she did. While many students had felt that the lecture had been both demanding and to those who found it too demanding, irrelevant, Anna saw the lecture as stimulating and more importantly the lecturer as a role model. The lecturer was not dismissed as being more able or more gifted, but as a future possibility; an inspirational figure who was simply at a later stage of her professional life and her professional development. For Anna she represented an alternative option, a possible-Anna projected into the future.

What do you think I mean by 'a possible-Anna'?

Here is my answer. The poet Robert Frost writes about 'the road not taken' the last three lines of which are:

> Two roads diverged in a wood, and I—
> I took the one less traveled by,
> And that has made all the difference. (Frost, accessed 2014)

Have you thought that your future isn't fixed and that you spend your time making, or at least trying to make, decisions which influence how your future will develop? That is what I mean by a 'future Anna'; so for 'Anna' put in your own name.

Now ask yourself, why did you or do you want to become a teacher? Who or what in your life influenced your decision?

As for Anna, this was not the only person of whom she spoke in such enthusiastic terms. When I visited her in school during her first year of teaching she said:

> So my mentor here is . . . oh she is just a fantastic teacher, so enthusiastic about teaching, she has been teaching probably only, I think it's only, five or six years, and so she's sort of relatively new to the profession, and still will teach a really creative lesson, really exciting, and I got the chance to come in, and she had my class last year, so she sort of passed them on to me, so I got the chance to come in and spend a few days with her in the class, and just see what she did with them, and what she did was fantastic, and I just sat there thinking that's what I'm going to be like next year. That's what teaching really is like.

Do you feel breathless reading that? I did hearing it. Notice also that Anna is speaking here about her mentor. Hold that thought for a moment and I'll come back to it.

When I asked Anna about why she had wanted to teach, she told me that at school her class had been visited by a Christian Aid worker 'who spoke enthusiastically about his work experiences in Nicaragua'. She was about thirteen at the time and said that she had been equally impressed by his tan but beyond that she had determined to do something similar when she was old enough. As she did Spanish as one of her languages at school, 5 years later she took a gap year working in an orphanage in Mexico. Clearly she did some good there, but she had of course gained something herself. She was more confident, more able to cope with difficulties (that is, she was more resilient which is perhaps why she understood the lecturer) her Spanish was more fluent and, most important of all, of course, she got a really good tan.

Think back of your earlier life. Who are your role models? What was it about them that stays with you and that you want to emulate? If you are in training or are now teaching – look around you, who do you look to now for inspiration? Now look wider still. Look outside of university or school to the wider world and your wider life. Which individuals set you a challenge and provide you your personal goals?

Looking at Anna's story it appears that she often saw individuals that she might emulate, who provided her with role models. However, here we return to the issue of her mentor because there is 'some overlap between the concepts of role model and mentors, critical distinctions also exist' (Murrell et al. 1999: 116). While the statutory regulations regarding the provision of 'mentors' is changing – where they remain they are now officially termed 'Induction Tutors' (Department for Education 2013), effective organizations still retain staff who perform this vital function not because of government statute but because they want to retain good practice and remain effective organizations. But even at the time of writing, while there may be a generic mentoring role in schools, it is perceived differently and consequently acted out differently by individuals in their own institutions (Sundli 2007). It is this diversity, not least in local terminology, which can lead to confusion when reading the research literature (Hennissen et al. 2008). However in this story, it is the distinction between the mentor and role model which is important. Mentors within the context of the English educational system have been developed as part of the school's organizational hierarchy and part of the transitional induction processes. They support a trainee's move into a full-time role of teacher. In fact, many organizations have developed mentoring far beyond this specific purpose.

What is your experience of mentors? What functions do they perform? If your experience is positive, what has made it so?

Here is one possible view from Andy Roberts who suggests that:

> mentoring appears to have the essential attributes of: a process; a supportive relationship; a helping process; a teaching-learning process; a reflective process; a career development process; a formalized process; and a role constructed by or for a mentor. The contingent attributes of the mentoring phenomenon appear as: coaching; sponsoring; role modelling; assessing; and an informal process.
> (Roberts 2000: 145)

In the context of this story Anna's mentor acts in the ways that Roberts has suggested but she also acts as a buffer or in Audrey Murrell's phrase 'run(ning) interference' (Murrell 2007) between the external pressures of local and national initiatives and inspection accountability and Anna's early career development. She specifically provides opportunities for Anna to become safely visible in the school, for example, by supporting her participation in staff meetings and school development sessions. And she models what Anna sees as good teaching. But remember, the mentor role model differs in quite a fundamental way from that of a role model. The mentor performs a specific function in the school, whereas as Gibson and Cordova suggest, the role model is constructed by the individual 'because identification resides in the head of the beholder and interaction may or may not be a component of the role modelling relationship', so it is that the beholder 'makes [a] role model by a conscious cognitive process of selectively viewing and assimilating desired attributes' (in Murrell et al. 1999: 116–17). So it is that the individual selects various aspects of one or a range of individuals to create 'new amalgams' (Bandura 1977: 48) that differ from any single individual, so that, 'the resulting behaviours may in fact be characterized by considerable novelty as well as emulation' (Murrell et al. 1999: 115–17).

A core issue for you as either a serving or aspiring teacher is not that you want or try to be a role model but that other people, including the children you work with, will create their own role models by drawing on various aspects of the people that they work with. Most of the times when you teach you do not know that this is happening. So it was when another teacher was told that the children in the local secondary school had been asked to identify their 'most inspiring teacher'; she was happy that one had identified her even though the teenager had been in her class 8 years before. You see, not only do you make your own role models from the people you meet; you in turn will serve to be a role model for future generations.

References and further reading

Bandura, A. (1977), *Social Learning Theory*. Englewood Cliffs, London: Prentice-Hall.

Department for Education (DfE) (2013), *Induction for Newly Qualified Teachers*, http://www.education. gov.uk/aboutdfe/statutory/g00212895/induction-nqts-england (accessed February 2014).

Frost, R. (2014), *The Road Not Taken*. http://www.poetryfoundation.org/poem/173536 (accessed February 2014).

Gibson, D. E. and Cordova, D. I. (1999), 'Women's and men's role models: The importance of exemplars', in A. J. Murrell, F. J. Crosby, and R. J. Ely (eds), *Mentoring Dilemmas: Developmental Relationships within Multicultural Organizations*. Mahwah, NJ: Lawrence Erlbaum Associates, 121–41.

Hennissen, P., Crasborn, F., Brouwer, N., Korthagen, F. and Bergen, T. (2008), 'Mapping mentor teachers' roles in mentoring dialogues', *Educational Research Review*, 3, 168–86.

Murrell, A. (2007), 'Five key steps for effective mentoring relationship', *The Kaitz Quarterly*, 1, 1–9.

Murrell, A., Crosby, F. and Ely, R. (1999), *Mentoring Dilemmas: Developmental Relationships within Multicultural Organizations*. Mahwah, NJ: Lawrence Earlbaum.

Roberts, A. (2000), 'Mentoring revisited: A phenomenological reading of the literature', *Mentoring and Tutoring*, 8, 145–70.

Sundli, L. (2007), 'Mentoring—A new mantra for education?', *Teaching and Teacher Education*, 23, 201–14.

A few good men: Why do so few men choose a career in primary education?

31

Jason Mellor

Recent government figures show that only around one-fifth of the students currently training to teach in primary schools in England are male (Department for Education 2012), while less than 15 per cent of the registered workforce in English primary schools are men (Warwick et al. 2012). If we accept the assumption that the teaching profession should reflect the diversity of the community within which it operates, then we must treat this significant imbalance as problematic. Indeed, if the context here was wildlife, we would be talking about an endangered species! This is not a recent phenomenon. The recruitment and retention of male primary school teachers has consistently been on the 'requires improvement' list for successive UK governments, professional and academic groups and has been the subject of significant ongoing media attention.

What are you initial thoughts about why this imbalance exists?

Although a review of the recent research within this area proposes a number of possible reasons for such a gender imbalance within primary education, there are three key themes which emerge consistently from the literature; 'social stereotyping', 'suspicion about the motives of male teachers' and 'a sense of male isolation'. These will be further examined in this chapter.

It could be argued that social stereotyping is a factor which contributes to the lack of men within primary schools. I have personal experience here. I remember being out for the evening with a group of male friends and the conversation turned to the challenges of work. While one of my peers discussed the complexity of dealing with some of his patients in the surgery and another discussed the challenge of 'removing' underperforming staff, I spoke about the difficulties faced when managing the behaviour of a particularly tricky class of 10–11-year-olds. Despite acknowledging that it was not a role that he would welcome himself, one of the group joked that teaching was 'a good job for the wife'. While I did challenge this perception, there is wider evidence to suggest that primary teaching is perceived to be a female-friendly profession

(Edmonds et al. 2002), with a relatively low status and the perceived notion that it provides a secure secondary household wage (Cushman 2005) rather than a primary income. While some may argue that we have moved on from the time-honoured notion that females are more caring, sensitive and creative than men (Mistry and Sood 2013), others argue that traditional beliefs about the qualities of men as 'breadwinners, managers, disciplinarians and not carers' (Smyth 2012, in Hepburn 2013: 1) are still commonly held within society.

To what extent do you agree with the claim that teaching in a primary school is a low-status, female-friendly profession?

While some men may be deterred by entrenched social stereotypes about the nature of primary teaching and the role of men within society, other writing identifies societal suspicion and concern about the motives of men seeking to work with young children. While some talk of the 'cloud of suspicion that may hang over male teachers' (Foster and Newman 2005: 350), others argue that the fear of being labelled a paedophile is 'the single biggest deterrent' (Holley 2007: 3) to men who would otherwise consider a career as a primary school teacher. Although it has been suggested that men have concerns about the perceived links between the caring nature of the teacher and child protection issues (Cushman 2005; Skelton 2007), a more recent study has suggested that while these anxieties are real, they are of concern to both male and female trainee teachers and are, therefore, not gender specific (Szwed 2010).

Do male and female trainees/teachers perceive issues relating to safeguarding, child protection or physical contact with children differently? If so, why might that be?

Perhaps one of the most significant factors which serves to discourage men from becoming primary school teachers is, ironically, the lack of other men in the profession. It may be a classic 'chicken and egg' situation! Indeed, male isolation is often reported as a concern both within initial teacher training and subsequently during the careers of male teachers (Thornton and Bricheno 2006). One trainee teacher described his experience as the only male in a small school as feeling like 'the freak show' (Warwick et al. 2012: 58); both the centre of attention as an anomalous male but also an outsider on the 'periphery' (Thornton and Bricheno 2006: 100) at the same time. Such complex juggling of multiple identities, in addition to developing the skills and competencies required as a class teacher, may present men with significant challenges which go beyond those faced by their female counterparts.

With a shortage of male role models within school, it has been suggested that some male teachers can lack 'mirrors' (Warwick 2012: 67) through which they are able to critically reflect on their own developing practice and professional identity. As a consequence, they may struggle to see a range of possible interpretations and incarnations of their role and ways in which it is possible to be a man in the primary classroom (Thomas 2006). Without such opportunities, it has been suggested that male teachers may experience an identity crisis or, at the very least, 'uncertainty and discomfort' (Jones 2007: 180).

To what extent do you agree with the suggestion that teachers benefit from gender role models to support their developing practice and professional identity? Does gender matter or is it really just about working alongside high-calibre colleagues?

It has been my own experience as a male primary school teacher that while gender may be an issue at times, especially in relation to some of the three key themes discussed within this chapter, issues associated with gender become less important and less visible over time. Instead, they are displaced by a rather more gender-neutral professional identity – one based on competence as a practitioner and commitment to the learning of the children alongside whom you work. However, it is my fear that many men that would make outstanding primary practitioners either leave the profession during or soon after their training, or perhaps never even consider the role in the first place. As a result, the male primary school teacher may be destined to remain an endangered species for the foreseeable future.

References and further reading

Cushman, P. (2005), 'Let's hear it from the males: Issues facing male primary school teachers', *Teaching and Teacher Education,* 21, (3), 227–40.

Department for Education (2012), *Record Numbers of Men Teaching in Primary Schools,* https://www.gov.uk/government/news/record-numbers-of-men-teaching-in-primary-schools-but-more-still-needed (accessed March 2014).

Edmonds, S., Sharp, C. and Benefield, P. (2002), *Recruitment to and Retention on Initial Teacher Training: A Systematic Review.* Windsor: NFER.

Foster, T. and Newman, E. (2005), 'Just a knock back? Identity bruising on the route to becoming a male primary school teacher', *Teachers and Teaching,* 11, (4), 341–58.

Hansen, P. and Mulholland, J. (2005), 'Caring and elementary teaching: The concerns of male beginning teachers', *Journal of Teacher Education,* 56, (2), 119–31.

Hepburn, H. (2013), 'Anxious times for male teachers in primary', *TES Connect,* http://www.tes.co.uk/article.aspx?storycode=6319996 (accessed March 2014).

Holley, G. (2007), *The Quiet Conspiracy: Men in Primary Schools,* http://i.telegraph.co.uk/multimedia/archive/00787/Graham_Holley_s_let_787315a.pdf (accessed March 2014).

Jones, D. (2007), 'Millennium man: Constructing identities of male teachers in early years' contexts', *Educational Review,* 59, (2), 179–94.

Mistry, M. and Sood, K. (2013), 'Why are there still so few men within early years in primary schools? Views from male trainee teachers and male leaders', *Education 3-13: International Journal of Primary, Elementary and Early Years Education,* 41, (1), 1–13.

Skelton, C. (2007), 'Gender, policy and initial teacher education', *Gender and Education,* 19, (6), 677–90.

Smyth, G. in Hepburn , H. (2013), 'Anxious times for male teachers in primary', *TES Connect,* http://www.tes.co.uk/article.aspx?storycode=6319996 (accessed March 2014).

Szwed, C. (2010), 'Gender balance in primary initial teacher education: Some current perspectives', *Journal of Education for Teaching: International Research and Pedagogy,* 36, (3), 303–17.

Thomas, K., (2006), '"Please can we have a man?": Male trainee English teachers entering predominantly female English departments', *Changing English: Studies in Culture and Education,* 13, (1), 137–50.

Thornton, M. and Bricheno, P. (2006), *Missing Men in Education.* Stoke on Trent: Trentham Books.

Warwick, J., Warwick, P. and Hopper, B. (2012), 'Primary teacher trainee perspectives on a male-only support group: Moving male trainee teachers beyond the "freak show"', *Teacher Development: An International Journal of Teachers' Professional Development,* 16, (1), 55–76.

Do teachers play it safe? 32
Rebecca Austin

When I was training to teach in the late 1980s, a rumour circulated (almost certainly apocryphal) about a student teacher who, in an attempt to stimulate a class of primary school children to more adventurous creative writing, put raw liver in a 'feely box'. The children lowered their hands into the darkened box and had to describe what they felt and then make up a story to match. The legend continues that the work produced by the children (particularly the boys – but that's a different discussion point!) was among some of the best, the most descriptive, they had ever done. I can come up with at least ten reasons off the top of my head why primary school teachers today (as they did 30 years ago) would say that was not a good idea. But it does sound like quite an exciting lesson and according to the story it did get results!

What is the motivation to teach such 'exciting' lessons? More importantly, what is the motivation NOT to teach them? To what extent are teachers prepared to take risks with their teaching? And what is it that counts as 'risky' teaching anyway?

A much-cited reason for playing it safe is the eponymous: 'health and safety' card. But it is the case that many schools' Health and Safety policies go beyond what is required by law and schools appear to have developed 'risk averse' cultures (Huggins and Wickett 2011). For example, in countries other than England it is quite the norm for children to play outdoors unsupervised in childcare settings and there is a growing consensus that opportunities for unsupervised outdoor play within communities should be maximized because of the perceived benefits to children's health and well-being (Hope et al. 2007). Even a supervising adult cannot prevent all risk of harm – accidents happen! It is interesting to consider why such caution is applied in school and daycare settings; perhaps increasing fear of litigation plays a part?

As long as reasonable precautions are taken to militate against the children coming to harm, should we not be open to the idea of children playing outside without being under the constant gaze of an adult?

Schools are seen as acting in *loco parentis* but perhaps most take on the super-cautious, over-protective parenting role rather than being the kind of parent who encourages the development of children's self-regulation of potentially risky behaviours?

I was chatting to a parent on the playground at the end of the school day a few years ago. She was ignoring the plaintive cries of her son who, bored, had climbed a tree by the school gate and had got himself stuck. Eventually, irritated by the interruption, she turned and called to him, 'If you got yourself up there, then you can get yourself down.' And sure enough he could! Rather than this being the attitude of a callous, uncaring parent, this was an attitude which demonstrated knowledge of her child, faith in his ability and the desire to foster independent problem-solving skills.

As a teacher in school is this how you see the children with whom you work – do you trust them to be able to handle themselves when faced with potential risk? What might this look like in the school setting?

In schools we sometimes find the desire to protect children cuts into the experiences we feel are appropriate for them. In my role in teacher education I have frequently had impassioned discussions with student teachers about what constitutes suitable reading material for children;

'They should only read books with happy endings' said one.

'Children don't need to read about the horrible things in life' said another.

The latter student was objecting to some books I had brought in to show them which dealt, through fiction, with the lives of children living through war and violence. An alternative perspective, which I tried to offer, was that reading such texts enables children to gain a wider picture of lives lived outside their own experience; and that they could do this from the 'safe distance' (Bettelheim 1978) of a story.

Do children need to be protected from the nastiness of life? Or do we need to find ways in which we can support them in understanding the reality of the world in which they live? What is the risk we take if we are willing to use material which might challenge, disturb or upset children?

Risky lessons often take an extra bit of effort in the planning and preparation stages. The pragmatist looks at the effort and asks if it is worth it. There is always the chance, if you are doing something you have not done before, or something that requires lots of things to come together, that it will not work. And if that happens, all your hard work will be for naught. At this point, the cautious (and busy) teachers throw up their hands and decide that a paper-and-pencil task or a tried-and-tested lesson will do the job just as well.

What about you? Will the thrill of the possibility of teaching a lesson which children will remember for the rest of their lives be enough for you to take the risk that they might remember it for all the wrong reasons?

Being a teacher is an intensely personal thing. It is founded on relationships which are about who you are and how you relate to others (that is why it is so difficult when others make judgements about our teaching; they are, in part, making judgements about us as people). But alongside our personal identity sits our professional identity – the kind of teacher we are and what we believe it means to be a teacher. In reflecting on what counts as risk, we weigh up what we do from both of these perspectives. The risk of what we do in the classroom might be considered a professional risk; something that might lead to you being seen as a particular kind of teacher; or it might be considered a personal risk, something that takes you out of your personal comfort zone in relation to who you are as a person.

We all have our own internal 'riskometer'. What is risky for you might be a walk in the park for someone else and vice versa. As a teacher we might take a professional risk on the balance we strike between teaching 'to the test' and teaching 'creatively'. As a person we might take a risk by using drama as a pedagogical tool for the very first time or by volunteering to run an after school juggling club or even putting liver in a box!

Do you play it safe? What does risky teaching look like to you?

References and further reading

Austin, R. (ed.) (2007), *Letting the Outside In: Developing Learning and Teaching Beyond the Early Years Classroom*. Stoke-on-Trent: Trentham.

Bettelheim, B. (1978), *The Uses of Enchantment: The Power and Importance of Fairy tales*. Harmondsworth: Penguin.

Buckingham, D. (1998), *Teaching Popular Culture: Beyond Radical Pedagogy*. London: Routledge.

Driscoll, P., Lambirth, A. and Roden, J. (eds) (2011), *The Primary Curriculum: A Creative Approach*. London: Sage.

Grainger, T. and Cremin, M. (2001), *Resourcing Classroom Drama: 5-8*. London: NAT.

Hope, G., Austin, R., Dismore, H., Hammond, S. and Whyte, T. (2007), 'Wild woods or urban jungle: Playing it safe or freedom to roam', *Education 3-13*, 35, (4), 321–32.

Huggins, V. and Wickett, K. (2011), 'Crawling and toddling in the outdoors', in S. Waite (ed.), *Children Learning Outside the Classroom from Birth to Eleven*. London: Sage, 2–19.

Knight, S. (2011), *Risk and Adventure in Early Years Outdoor Play: Learning from Forest Schools*. London: Sage.

Robinson, K. (2011), *Out of Our Minds: Learning to Be Creative*. Chichester: Capstone.

Waite, S. (ed.) (2011), Children Learning Outside the Classroom from Birth to Eleven. London: Sage.

Endnote

We hope that this book, alongside the previous publication, *Developing Teacher Expertise*, has raised some issues about aspects of teaching and learning in the primary classroom. Nothing is absolute about Education; it evolves, as does your own professional practice. As we become more aware of educational practices around the world and are required to meet the demands of an ever more complex society, teaching has become increasingly demanding and our teaching practices are more closely scrutinized.

Every teacher is unique and that is their strength. They draw upon many sources for their professional practice and a part of teacher development is to continue to be informed about current research and policy; but not only to know about it but also to reflect on the implications for their own teaching. It is challenging to change one's practice in the highly pressurized schools of today but if it benefits children's learning it is worth doing.

Index